Therapists Praise *Taming Marital Arguments: Breaking Out of the T.R.A.P.*

"Dr. Rugel offers a thoughtful and practical approach to acknowledging, assessing, interrupting, and redirecting destructive patterns of marital communication while honoring the dignity of the individual by respecting past life experiences which influence each partner's underlying beliefs, assumptions, and thought processes."

Holli Kenley M.A. MFT, Author
Breaking Through Betrayal: And Recovering The Peace Within

"In *Taming Marital Arguments*, Dr. Rugel takes the reader through a maze of how not to engage in destructive dialogue which may lead to the T.R.A.P. sequence and its ensuing conflict. In his book, Rugel presents a well-rounded approach of communication exercises, case discussions, and detailed instruction for couples. His foundation in interpersonal skills is aptly used and shines to illuminate this relationship psychology book with compassion and enlightenment."

Barbara Sinor, Ph.D., Author
Tales of Addiction and Inspiration for Recovery

"Marital arguments are symptoms of the deep-set malaise that grips the vast majority of marriages only a few years into these onerous and unnatural arrangements. This book is one of the most level-headed looks at nuptial discord. It offers, in equal measures, compassion, unflinching observation, and practical advice, all wrapped in a thorough investigation of why erstwhile lovers, mates, and partners turn into hateful, inanely bickering enemies. Like their political counterparts, marital arguments are bitter and uncompromising precisely because they pack a wallop of emotions and common history. The book first disentangles the web of expectations and self-deceit that underlie conjugal contracts and then proceeds methodically to unravel the intricate network of wounds and triggers that give rise to fights and shouting matches in marriage.

The book proceeds from an overview of self-feeding and self-reflecting marital dynamics to an exposition of the role in the bond of the psychology of the partners, especially if they are bent on avoiding a repeat of earlier traumas and pain. A variety of emotions, counter-emotions, traits, and behaviors contribute to the breakdown of communications and, consequently, of marriages. The author does a superb job of analyzing them all and, thus, demonstrating why partners are sometimes perceived by their nearest and dearest to be threatening and subversive rather than nurturing and supportive. To sidestep such pitfalls, the author advocates enhanced self-awareness and self-administered behavior modification and provides the tools to accomplish these goals. The book is most helpfully interspersed with examples of arguments and fights between couples and how to resolve them productively as well as questionnaires and tests.

Taming Marital Arguments is proof that a book should never be judged by the number of its pages. It packs into its slender spine more punch and value for money than many a thickset textbooks about couples and their communication problems. An absolute delight!"

Sam Vaknin, PhD, author
Malignant Self-love: Narcissism Revisited

Taming Marital Arguments: Breaking Out of the T.R.A.P.

THE COUPLE DEFEATS TRAPPER

Robert P. Rugel, PhD

Library of Congress Cataloging-in-Publication Data

Rugel, Robert P.
  Taming marital arguments : breaking out of the T.R.A.P. / by Robert P.
Rugel ; foreword by Sandra L. Ceren.
      p. cm. -- (New horizons in therapy series)
  Includes bibliographical references and index.
  ISBN-13: 978-1-61599-019-1 (trade paper : alk. paper)
  ISBN-10: 1-61599-019-4 (trade paper : alk. paper)
  ISBN-13: 978-1-61599-020-7 (case laminate : alk. paper)
  ISBN-10: 1-61599-020-8 (case laminate : alk. paper)
  1. Marital conflict. 2. Married people--Psychology. 3. Marital psycho-
therapy. I. Title.
  HQ734.R796 2010
  646.7'8--dc22
                                    2009049535

Distributed by: Ingram Book Group, Bertram's Books, New Leaf
Distributing.

Published by
Loving Healing Press, Inc.
5145 Pontiac Trail
Ann Arbor, MI 48105

www.LHPress.com
info@LHPress.com

Tollfree USA/CAN: 888-761-6268
Fax 734-663-6861

Contents

Table of Figures

Exercises

Exercises

Foreword

In Taming *Marital Arguments: Breaking out of the T.R.A.P.* Dr. Robert P. Rugel, a highly experienced marital psychologist utilizes his clinical acumen to illuminate the causes and dynamics of marital discord and offers an easy- to-read instructive path away from conflict and toward resolution. Numerous case examples covering an array of marital problems with which couples can readily identify enliven the book.

Utilizing his innovative T.R.A.P. sequence Dr. Rugel demonstrates how and why arguments start and escalate. This method should help propel couples towards understanding the reasons and origins of their conflict and how to stop its progression.

He rightly points out that marriages are threatened and may be doomed when partners experience a lack of support, communication avoidance, selfishness, criticism, derogation, control, coercion, dominance, withdrawal, anger, insecurity, disregard, jealousy, lying, keeping secrets and lack of responsibility.

In my pre-marital work spanning forty years, I frequently counsel divorced people who appear determined not to make the same mistake again. Their previous marriages failed for many of reason that Dr. Rugel discusses. With good cause, some people may question their ability to determine if their current partner is an appropriate choice for a spouse. Sometimes they select someone who resembles the previous mate in personality or appearance or in the negative way in which they relate to others. In such cases they need a reminder of the dangerous behaviors that Dr. Rugel states can destroy a marriage.

Most healthy people are eager for a satisfying relationship in which they feel "at home" with one another and where they can regard themselves as the other's best friend. In this climate of comfort and security the couple can develop a good, dependable, trustworthy and caring relationship.

To help couples struggling in their marriage, Rugel presents exercises to help them assess and monitor their own threatening behavior and recognize the "choice point" and consider the consequences. This is a recipe for healthy change.

Couples in conflict and the professionals who treat them should find the vignettes and exercises helpful as a road map to navigate away from conflict and towards building a strong, emotionally secure marriage.

Sandra Levy Ceren, PhD

Dr. Ceren's credentials include: Diplomate in Marital Therapy, American Board of Family Psychology, and Fellow, Academy of Family Psychology. She is the author of *Essentials of Premarital Counseling: Creating Compatible Couples* and *Look Before You Leap: A Premarital Guide for Couples*.

Preface

In marriage, unfortunately, people are often blind to the consequences of their own negative behavior. They say and do things that will come back to haunt them, but they cannot see what is happening. This is one of the sad realities of marital life. When, as a consequence of their own behavior, they are treated badly by their partners, they feel hurt, victimized, and confused.

A memorable example in the author's experience concerned a wife who, in a moment of anger, slapped her husband and scratched his face. Moments later she regretted her action and wanted a hug. When he refused, she felt hurt and victimized. The situation was the culmination of many negative interactions between them that both had contributed to. Neither was without blame. But the bottom line is simple: *you can't slap someone in the face and then expect a hug.* This may seem obvious, but in troubled marriages nothing is obvious.

Another example concerned a man who had experienced a series of relationships that followed the same negative pattern and had the same unhappy ending. "Why does this always happen to me?" he said in a confused and mournful way. He wanted to understand. But he was unable to ask himself the key question: "Do I in some way contribute to what happens to me? Am I the author of my own experience?" This is a difficult question for people to ask themselves. And when they have the courage to ask it, they find that the answer does not come easily. Life is complicated and unpredictable. However, if we look hard enough, we can recognize some of the ways we contribute to the emotional climate that we live in.

This process plays itself out in many unhappy marriages that are plagued by escalating arguments. Because arguing causes us to feel threatened and emotionally upset, when we argue we lose the ability to see what is going on. In our state of defensiveness we cannot see how we are contributing to the escalation of hurtful interactions. The author calls these arguments TRAP sequences. The acronym TRAP stands for (T)threaten (R)eact (A)nd (P)rotect. When both spouses feel threatened, react, and protect themselves, they become caught in a vicious negative cycle from which neither can escape.

It doesn't have to be this way. Hopefully, this book will help you recognize this dangerous pattern and learn to avoid it.

1	**Using the TRAP Sequence to Understand Arguments**

Fig. 1-1: Trapper controlling the couple

The TRAP Sequence

It takes three steps to create a marital argument:

- Step 1: The triggering spouse says or does something that hurts the partner's feelings. The triggering spouse is usually unaware that he or she has done something hurtful to the partner.
- Step 2: The partner reacts to this hurt by doing something self-protective. Sometimes it is an accusation, at other times it is withdrawal. Whatever it is, it now threatens the triggering spouse's feelings.
- Step 3: The triggering spouse now reacts defensively to the partner, usually in a way that again threatens the partner.

Following these three steps, both are emotionally upset, thus creating the essential ingredients for an escalating argument. I call these three steps a TRAP sequence because couples become trapped in this pattern of action and reaction and can't escape from it. They repeat it again and again until each is so threatened by the other that they become enemies.

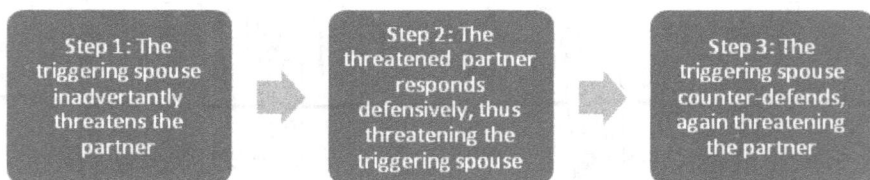

Step 1: The triggering spouse inadvertantly threatens the partner		Step 2: The threatened partner responds defensively, thus threatening the triggering spouse		Step 3: The triggering spouse counter-defends, again threatening the partner

Fig. 1-2: The TRAP Sequence

To avoid arguments you must become aware of the futility of this pattern. If you and your partner continue to argue until you become enemies, your marriage will be ruined. Unfortunately, this happens quite often. We start out as lovers and friends, but end up as enemies.

Avoiding this fate is more difficult than you might think. We human beings are hard-wired by evolution to identify enemies and to protect ourselves from them. This is how we survived as a species. As a result we can easily come to perceive our partner as the enemy and to engage in defensive behaviors that cause our partners to feel likewise.

Consider what happened to Jim and Carol:

Jim and Carol had been arguing for weeks. They had become each other's enemy and were distrustful of one another. In Jim's attempt to fix things, he had spent the day preparing a meal for Carol. He carefully chose the menu, the wine, and the glassware. He wanted everything to be perfect. The meal began with them both in good spirits as Jim ladled squash onto Carol's plate. Carol indicated when there was enough squash. The squash did not look right to Jim. There was too much green and not enough yellow. He wanted it to be perfect. Jim added two more pieces of yellow squash to balance out the color on her plate. Jim did not realize that he had just initiated Step 1.

Carol felt that Jim was ignoring her. She had said there was enough squash and he had not listened. She didn't like the feeling of being ignored. It made her feel small, like she was not worth listening to. Carol initiated Step 2 when she took an action to get rid of this bad feeling. In an annoyed voice Carol said there was enough squash. She didn't want anymore. She then added, "You never listen to me. Maybe we shouldn't be together anymore!"

Jim was shocked. She was talking about leaving. In an instant all his efforts had blown up in his face. Now Jim felt accused and upset. Before he realized it he responded defensively. He said, "You never appreciate anything I do for you!" Now both were upset. They ended up in one of their old arguments. The meal was ruined.

What happened? How could something start out so well and be ruined so quickly? This book will help you understand why. Arguing occurs because spouses can easily threaten the self-esteem and security of the partner. Some spouses may appear on the surface to be thick-skinned, but, in reality, most people are sensitive and easily upset.

When a spouse's self-esteem or security is threatened, that person will automatically become defensive. The way the spouse becomes defensive will usually be equally threatening to the partner. When *both* spouses become defensive at the same time, all hell can break lose.

Many couples want to avoid arguing. They just don't know how to do it. The solutions provided in this book are simple, but they are not easy. The first and most important solution is to avoid Step 1. *Avoid making your partner feel threatened and you will avoid destructive arguing!* The second is harder, but still possible. It is to find a way to remain non-defensive in the face of threat. If you can remain calm, you can find a way out of the argument. In this book we will describe how to do this. We will teach you to: (1) recognize a TRAP sequence; (2) understand the futility of the TRAP sequence; and, (3) learn how to avoid the TRAP sequence.

What Do People Want? Beyond the Romantic Stage

When spouses marry they are usually in the romantic stage of their relationship. They feel loved in each other's presence. They make each other feel wonderful. The couple wants to spend every moment together. Excitement, euphoria, and sexual energy abound. They assume it will always be that way. If you asked them what they want in their marriage, they will mention love, romance, great sex, companionship, adventure, a supportive family, and the hope of building an exciting life together.

If you were to say to them, "What you should be trying to do is create a safe relationship that is free from threat and arguing," they would probably reply, "Well of course, but we already have that." And indeed they do have that. The challenge is to keep it when their needs begin to clash and they begin dealing with their differences. The clash of differing needs challenges most marriages.

The Downside of Romance

The way your partner makes you feel wonderful is the upside of the romantic stage. The down side is that since your partner can make you feel wonderful, he or she can also take that feeling away and make you feel miserable. This can occur during moments of frustration when you and your partner begin to differ about what you want and when you try to negotiate your differences. If during that negotiation you feel disregarded by your partner, the change from wonderful to miserable begins. Unless spouses can minimize acts of disregard and the arguing that follows, all of the exciting expectations about marriage will be dashed.

The Clash of Spousal Needs and Marital Deterioration

Spouses are not clones of one another. They will differ about what they want to eat; at what temperature to set the thermostat; how often to have sex; who will do the laundry; how they will spend their money; or how to parent their kids. In the course of a day there are hundreds of small and large situations where our needs differ from those of our partner.

Successful Attempts at Solving the Clash of Needs

Solving the clash of needs begins when both partners can discuss their differences with mutual regard and without frustration. Spouses know they will not always get what they want, and they are often willing to give up what they want if during the discussion they feel that they have been taken seriously. If each spouse manages to convey that he or she is taking the partner's wishes seriously, the issue will probably be resolved with neither feeling threatened.

Couples who can do this will save themselves considerable marital grief. Unfortunately, not all spouses are able to do this. During a clash many spouses become frustrated, forget about the needs and feelings of the partner, and push for what they want.

One-Sided Attempts to Solve the Clash of Needs

Many of us *want what we want when we want it,* and become frustrated when we don't get it. When frustrated, we often become oblivious to our partner's feelings and needs. In our attempts to get what we want, we often become insensitive. We coerce, criticize, or manipulate to get what we want, oblivious to the needs and feelings of our partners. Our partners may do likewise. They too *want what they want when they want it.*

The Moment of Emotional Pain: My Partner Doesn't Care

During the clash of needs, if the spouse notices that the partner repeatedly does not seem to have his or her interests in mind, the tension begins to mount. The spouse may not notice this at first. During the romantic stage we ignore most negative aspects of our partner's character. But as time goes on we begin to keep score and we begin to feel resentment. We think to ourselves, "Is my partner aware of me? Does my partner care about me?" These thoughts threaten our self-esteem and our security. They are a far cry from the romantic stage when the feeling was "My partner loves me and makes me feel wonderful!"

If the clash of needs is repeatedly handled badly by spouses, with each pushing for his or her own interests at the expense of the partner, the initial positive perception of the partner begins to change. But it becomes even worse than that. We begin to feel not only that our partner is oblivious to our feelings, but also that our partner is thwarting us intentionally.

Perceiving Intentional Disregard

It is bad enough that spouses single-mindedly pursue their own interests at the expense of the partner. When we go further and conclude: "My partner is ignoring and frustrating me on purpose. She is doing this intentionally, to hurt me," then we have begun to distort reality. We think that our spouse, the person who can make us feel wonderful, is instead intentionally trying to hurt us.

Our partners may indeed be oblivious to our needs. But, unless there is a roaring argument going on, there is usually no intent to cause hurt. However, it seems that way to the spouse, who will then need to protect against the perceived enemy.

Consider John and Jill, whose many arguments have created mutual wariness. They are riding in the car and having an amiable conversation. Jill is cold and turns the heat up. John begins to feel hot and turns the heat down. Jill thinks to herself, "He is turning the heat down to spite me. He wants me to be uncomfortable. He is so mean." Suddenly, the good feelings vanish.

John may have been insensitive, but he was not intentionally trying to make Jill uncomfortable. However, as a result of her wariness, Jill has begun to misinterpret John's actions. To her, he has just been intentionally hurtful. Nothing he can say will convince her otherwise. Her misinterpretation makes the situation worse.

The *Feelings of Rejection Generator*: Finding Evidence for Rejection

When we experience intentional disregard, we begin to think that our partners are unkind, cold, or overbearing. Words like "selfish," "jerk," or "bitch" begin to creep into our minds when we think about our partners. Once we begin to think this way, our partners become more threatening. Without realizing it, we begin to look for more evidence that these negative labels are true. Our *feeling rejected generators* begin to take over. The rejection generator causes us to find more evidence of bad treatment when, in fact, it is not there. The more evidence of rejection we find, the more threatening our partners seem.

Responding to Your Partner Like a Snake in the Woods

If our marital partners come to be identified as intentionally hurtful—as potential enemies—then we automatically respond to them with the same fight/flight emotional system that helped our ancestors deal with predators.

To understand this, consider a classic fear situation: encountering a snake in the woods. Imagine that you are walking in unfamiliar woods. You are lost and uncomfortable. Suddenly you see a snake. Since poisonous snakes can kill you, your emotional brain immediately takes over. When your emotional brain takes over, you no longer think, you react.

Your Mobilized Body

Instantaneously the emotional brain mobilizes the body to deal with the threat. It signals for the release of glucose and stress hormones to provide for greater energy and alertness. Your heart starts pumping faster, your muscles become tense, your blood pressure rises, your pupils dilate, and your perspiration increases. In your suddenly mobilized state you jump back reflexively to avoid the snake. This occurs in milliseconds. *You did not think—you just reacted. It just happened.* Similarly, in marriage, when you perceive your partner as the enemy, the emotional brain is activated. Automatically you react. Before you know it, you have said or done something. Usually it is something destructive.

In the woods, when the rest of your brain catches up to your less accurate, but faster, emotional brain, you can begin to think more clearly. You realize the snake was a branch. You quickly calm down. However, calming down is required because your emotional brain has prepared your body to deal with threat—a threat that in this case did not exist. When you calm down in marriage, you may realize that you over-reacted, but the damage is already done.

Overestimating Danger

The emotional brain behaves as though it is better to overestimate the presence of danger and calm down later than to underestimate danger, be bitten by a poisonous snake and die. This tendency to overestimate threat has unfortunate consequences in marriage. When threatened, we often misinterpret our partner's intent as more negative than it actually is, and we react defensively without thinking.

Memory Files

In the woods, if a snake is actually present, further changes occur. Our emotional brains tell the memory areas of our brains to retrieve snake relevant information: our experiences with garden snakes, poisonous snakes, and boa constrictors are all kept in memory files that are now activated. Our brains compare the present snake situation to these files to determine the degree of danger. We also have memory files for feeling disregarded or demeaned that are called up for comparison in threatening marital situations.

If significant danger is determined to be present, defensive action is initiated: usually flight. If we cannot run, we attack. We become focused on using whatever is available to ward off the snake or the threatening partner.

Storing the New Experience in Memory Files

When the threat is resolved, memories of the experience are encoded in our memory files. The databank on snakes or threatening spouses is enlarged. Our capacity to cope with future snake situations is enhanced. Unfortunately, our ability to cope with threatening marital situations is not enhanced.

Getting Bitten

Let's consider the worst circumstance. Our avoidance or attack maneuvers do not work and we are bitten by the snake. Now we have real harm to contend with. More stress hormones are pumped into the blood stream to deal with the crisis. Hopefully, in our wounded but mobilized state we are able to seek help and do what is necessary to survive.

The stress of a traumatic event like this will result in permanent changes in our memory centers. Walking in the woods will never be the same. It will forever be experienced as more threatening. When we enter the woods, our emotional brain will immediately be on alert. Our tendency to misread cues as evidence of a snake will increase. Out readiness to protect ourselves will be heightened.

The Instantaneous Reaction: We Respond to Our Partners as Snakes

Our partners cannot bite and kill us, but they can certainly hurt us emotionally. They can threaten our sense of self-worth and they can threaten our security. They can do this by ignoring us and making us feel unimportant; by criticizing us and make us feel inferior; by withdrawing from us and making us feel abandoned. All these experiences hurt.

The Moment of Emotional Pain

Within a millisecond of such a hurtful action, we experience a feeling that is painful. It may be momentary sense of shame or humiliation (I am not worth paying attention to); It may be guilt (I am a bad person); It may be a feeling of abandonment (I will be alone). These negative feelings occur instantly and we also deal with them instantly just as we deal with a snake in the woods. *We reflexively say and do self-protective things that we will later regret.*

Self-Protection

If this occurs repeatedly our partners become fixed in the role of the enemy. In our partner's presence we *stop thinking clearly and start reacting defensively.* We carefully scan for threat and find it whether it is really there or not. This only increases the number of painful emotional experiences that we must defend against. All of this will bring on TRAP sequences.

More on the Three Steps of The TRAP Sequence

A TRAP sequence consists of three steps:

Step 1: The Threatening Behavior.

The TRAP sequence begins when a spouse engages in a behavior that is threatening to the partner. Things may have gone well for several hours, days, or weeks, and then there will be a clash of needs. One spouse will want something when the other spouse wants something else. During this clash of needs the frustrated spouse may engage in an insensitive behavior such as a coercive act or an act of disregard that threatens the partner's self-esteem or security.

John was exhausted as he walked through the door at the end of the day. He wanted to relax. His wife, Jane, greeted him and said, "I need your help with the kids." In an abrupt and irritated voice he replied, "Leave me alone, I am tired!" Jane was also exhausted and was counting on his help. His comment caused her to feel ignored and unimportant. That hurt.

Step 2: The Defensive Reaction

Reacting defensively is Jane's automatic response to the threatening behavior. The partner whose self-esteem or security has been threatened does something protective to neutralize the painful emotion, in Jane's case, the feeling of being dismissed. This could be a blaming statement, an attack on the spouse's character, or a moment of cold withdrawal.

Jane's self-protective response helped to rid her of the hurtful feeling of being dismissed. She replied, "You never help me." How was this response helpful to Jane? The inference was clear. It is not that she was unworthy of being helped. Instead, it was that John is selfish. Her defensive reaction threatened John's self-esteem. John felt accused of selfishness, causing him a moment of emotional pain.

Step 3: The Defensive Counter-Reaction

A defensive counter-reaction is John's response to Jane's insinuation that he is selfish and bad.

To rid himself of the bad feelings of implied selfishness, John replied, "You are always demanding something!"

Now Jane has been accused of being demanding, thus leading to the next round in the escalating argument.

Negative Escalation

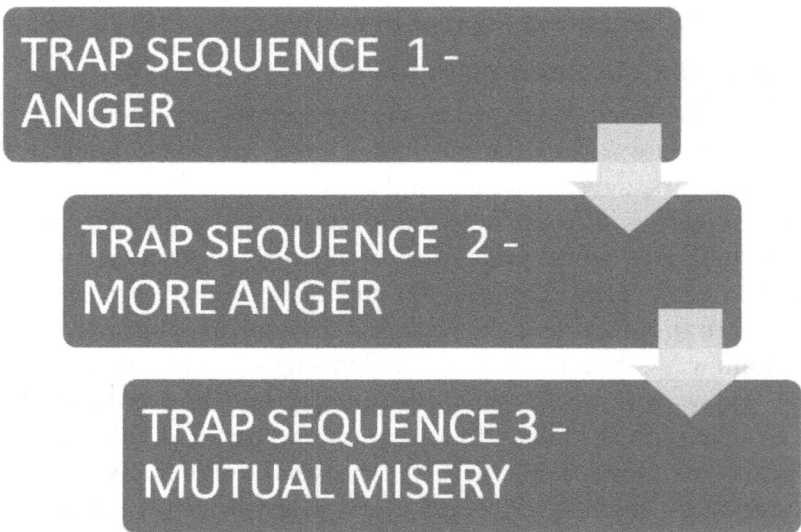

TRAP SEQUENCE 1 - ANGER

TRAP SEQUENCE 2 - MORE ANGER

TRAP SEQUENCE 3 - MUTUAL MISERY

Fig. 1-3: Negative Escalation

As each partner becomes increasingly defensive, the emotional intensity increases, and the interaction can get increasingly out of control. It ends with both spouses feeling wounded. If the pattern repeats itself often enough, it can become a death spiral for the marriage.

If the TRAP sequence were a musical piece, it would begin as a faint three note melody. The three note melody would repeat itself throughout the musical piece growing in intensity and complexity. At the end it would become ominous and thunderous. But the TRAP sequence is not a melody. Instead, it is a three step interaction between spouses that grows until it destroys the marriage.

Imagine That You Live In a Marital Bubble

Fig. 1-4: The Marital Bubble

If we spouses understood how sensitive our partners actually are, and how prone they are to feeling rejected, perhaps we would treat them with more care. Sadly, this is often not the case. Thus, we often treat our partners as though they were made of steel—impervious to hurt. We would be better off treating them like the human/fragile creatures they really are.

The problem of psychological threat becomes even greater because within marriage everything is intensified. If you think of marriage as existing within a bubble, perhaps this will become clearer. Imagine that, after marriage, a boundary surrounds you and your spouse. Spouses can't see it, but it is there. When spouses are at home, the bubble encloses them. When they leave the house to go to work or to be with friends, the bubble is still there. There is no escaping the bubbled existence that is marriage.

What we want within the bubble is a sense of self-worth and security. This depends on the love and responsiveness of our partners. When we get it, and when our partners get it, the bubble becomes bright, peaceful and harmonious. It becomes a safe refuge that helps maintain physical and emotional health.

Unfortunately, the invisible bubble that surrounds the couple magnifies everything negative that occurs within it. Slights or put-downs bounce off the bubble and return to the space between the spouses with intensified force. As a result, we spouses are even more vulnerable within the bubble. The bubble not only intensifies negative behaviors, it also preserves them. No fight or argument ever leaves the bubble. Memories of hurtful events live on indefinitely in the bubble.

Your behavior will be carefully scrutinized by your partner within the bubble. Every gesture will be evaluated by your partner for threat implications: Did that behavior mean that my partner loves me or dislikes me? Did it mean that my partner respects me or disrespects me? Did that mean that my partner wants to be with me or wants to avoid me?

Because you are so carefully observed within the bubble, you have tremendous power to influence your partner's feelings. You have the power to threaten your partner and you have the power to make your partner feel secure. It is true that if you are aware of this power, it can make living in the bubble feel like a burden. But if you are not aware of it, it can make living in the bubble feel like hell. If your spouse concludes "My partner doesn't love me, doesn't respect, doesn't want me," the bubble becomes dark, oppressive and scary.

2	# The Role of *Protector* # In TRAP Sequences

Fig. 2-1: Meet the Protector

To fully understand TRAP sequences you must understand *Protector*. *Protector* is the instinctive mechanism we humans have that helps us recognize and avoid pain. *Protector* helps with the threat of a snake. *Protector* also helps us to recognize a threat to our self-esteem or security in marriage.

Protector Personalizes and Asks: "Is This about Me?"

Personalizing is our automatic tendency to relate the upsetting events we experience to ourselves. In any distressing situation we humans will ask ourselves: "Is the situation relevant to me?" Doing so helps us determine if what we face is relevant to our survival. When a snake is present the conclusion drawn by *Protector* is "Yes, this is about me. It is about my safety. I must run or be bitten!"

In situations such as marriage, the question "Is this about me?" also occurs. However, in marriage, it becomes more complicated. It becomes, "Is this about my self-esteem or security? Am I being treated badly because of something within me, some flaw or inadequacy of mine? Is it my fault that I am being rejected?" This thought process takes place within milliseconds. The answer we provide ourselves also occurs within milliseconds.

Histories of Emotional Pain and the Current Moment

If the answer to the above question is: "Yes, this bad treatment means that I am unworthy or inadequate" then the emotional pain becomes worse. During the moment of emotional pain our entire history of hurtful experiences with others is reactivated. All of the moments when significant others caused us to feel unworthy or inadequate have been stored in the memory centers of our brains. These memories, as well as the associated painful feelings, remain inactive until suddenly re-activated by our current marital situation.

Some of us are fortunate. We have not had many moments of emotional pain. There is little in our past histories to become re-activated during the current moment of emotional pain. Others of us are not so lucky. We have had more than our share of emotional pain. We are primed by our histories to respond quickly and intensely when we feel hurt by our partners.

Protector Turns the "Me" Into a "You"

The moment of emotional pain doesn't last long for any of us because *Protector* will not allow it to. *Protector* helps us rid ourselves of painful feelings so quickly that often we don't even recognize what happened.

Protector helps reduce our pain by turning the "it is about me" into "it is about you." Psychologists call this externalizing. *Protector* puts the source of the painful feelings outside of us. *Protector* helps us conclude "this isn't happening to me because I am bad or unworthy. **The reason for the painful feelings I am having is my partner.** It is something bad within him or her that causes my pain."

Before we consider this process in marriage, let's consider how *Protector* operates outside of marriage.

Protector **Externalizes**

Consider the following examples with Jill and John. Jill and John both want to feel good about themselves; however, they are faced with circumstances that could make them feel otherwise. Consider how *Protector* helps them.

Jill Externalizes

In college, Jill had her heart set on joining a certain sorority. She went to the open houses, talked to the members, and made it clear that this was the sorority for her. But on the day that invitations went out, she did not receive one.

Jill felt rejected and inadequate. She was devastated. With the help of *Protector*, she externalized the problem. She concluded that it wasn't her, it was them. They were a bunch of stupid, superficial snobs. She began to feel better.

John Externalizes

John was a hardworking student. He had a great deal invested in being accepted into a certain prestigious college. His chances of getting in were ruined when he did not do well on the SATs. He was crushed. He felt ashamed. With the help of *Protector* he externalized the problem. He decided that it wasn't him, it was them. He concluded that the ETS Corporation creates meaningless, lousy tests. He began to feel better.

Outside the marital bubble *Protector* handles these situations well. This is mostly a good thing. When Jill or John externalize no one gets hurt. The sorority or ETS are not affected and Jill and John feel better.

We would be a lot worse off without *Protector*. *Protector* helps us create a benign world for ourselves that we can live in comfortably. That world may be somewhat skewed. It may not always correspond with the real world. But for the most part, it is a world that works for us.

Protector **and the TRAP Sequence**

Unfortunately, *Protector*'s methods backfire in marriage and *Protector* becomes the worst enemy of the relationship. *Protector*'s methods backfire because there are two *Protector*s in the marital bubble, each trying to defend their respective spouse by putting the problem onto the other. *Protector*'s method of externalizing, i.e. using accusations, blaming statements and "put-downs," inevitably creates TRAP sequences.

Let's backtrack and look at how *Protector* and the TRAP sequence operate in the family of origin.

Protector and the TRAP Sequence in Childhood

Consider big brother Jimmy and little sister Alison, who both want to think of themselves as good children. In the following situation the threatening event occurs when little sister Alison inadvertently bumps into big brother Jimmy's block tower, knocking it over. Jimmy believes that Alison has done this intentionally. This makes Alison the threatening enemy. In his angry state he blames Alison and yells at her. "You are bad," he says. He wants his mother to agree that Alison is bad. Alison will now have to engage in a defensive counter-reaction. Guided by her *Protector*, she will deny the accusation and counter-accuse saying, "I am not bad; you are bad!" The two siblings will then continue to blame and accuse, guided by their *Protector*s. Consider their interaction:

Jimmy says to mother: "Alison is mean. She knocked over my block tower."

Alison replies: "No, I didn't."

Jimmy replies loudly: "Yes, you did!"

The battle escalates.

Alison: "No, I didn't!"

Jimmy replies: "Yes, you did!"

Alison's Protector then tries a new strategy to avoid blame. She counter-accuses, attempting to shift blame to Jimmy.

Alison says: "You pushed me into it."

Jimmy's Protector now must help him avoid blame by denying the accusation.

Jimmy replies: "No, I didn't."

Alison relies: "Yes, you did!"

With the two *Protector*s active their battle will continue to escalate. Each *Protector* will shield its particular sibling by attacking the other. The mother will now intervene to break up the destructive pattern.

Protector in Marriage

When both *Protector*s are active in the marital bubble, spouses act no differently than children. However, in the martial bubble, there is no maternal figure to mediate the conflict. Consider Mr. and Mrs.

Jones. Mr. Jones' forgetfulness was a marital problem since he often forgot his wife's requests. Eventually she began to feel insulted by this, believing that, if he behaved this way, she could not be very important to him. This would often trigger a TRAP sequence.

One such instance involved the porch light. Sometimes Mrs. Jones visited her friends and came home late. She had repeatedly asked Mr. Jones to leave the porch light on for her. He repeatedly forgot. This made Mrs. Jones angry. Not only did it make finding the right key difficult, but his forgetting made Mrs. Jones felt like she wasn't important enough for him to remember. That hurtful feeling brought *Protector* into the situation. To get rid of the painful sense that she was unimportant to her husband, she turned the "me" into a "you" and made the accusation that he was thoughtless. This made her feel better—it wasn't that she was not worth being considered, it was that he thought only about himself.

Mr. and Mrs. Jones and the TRAP Sequence

Step 1: The Threatening Behavior
Mr. Jones forgot—the porch light was not on.
Step 2: The Defensive Reaction
Mrs. Jones felt disregarded. She turned the "me" into a "you."
Mrs. Jones (angrily): "You didn't turn the light on again. You *never* think about my feelings!"
Step 3: The Defensive Counter-Reaction
Her comment made Mr. Jones feel bad about himself. He had experienced this feeling before—the sense that he could never do anything right. Mr. Jones' *Protector* took over to shield him from his discomfort. Mr. Jones responded with a denial. He said: "That is not true. I am aware of your feelings."

Mrs. Jones has run into a stone wall. His denial makes Mrs. Jones feel disregarded and angrier. This results in another TRAP sequence and an escalating argument.

Protector is Not Very Bright

Protector is good at shielding people from pain, but in marriage its efforts only bring on more pain. *Protector* means well but is not very bright. *Protector* does not understand cause and effect. *Protector* cannot anticipate TRAP sequences. If Mr. Jones's *Protector* were smarter, it would understand that a better way to protect Mr. Jones from the pain of accusations would be to make sure the porch light is on, thus avoiding the TRAP sequence. Failing that, *Protector* could have Mr. Jones apologize. Alas, this is not something *Protector* can do. *Protector* can look for threat and defend against it. But *Protector* is not good at anticipating TRAP sequences or defusing them.

The key to avoiding arguments: To avoid the misery of TRAP sequences, spouses must come to understand what behaviors their partners find threatening and learn how to avoid those behaviors. This will keep *Protector* asleep. Life is much more pleasant when *Protector* is asleep.

If *Protector* Did Not Exist: Mr. and Mrs. Jones

Consider what marriage would be like without *Protector*. In the following example, Mrs. Jones complains about the porch light.

Mrs. Jones says to Mr. Jones: "I am not happy with you. You forgot to put on the porch light again. I want you be more aware of my feelings."

Mr. Jones didn't realize she felt this way. He begins to feel sorry for his wife. Wanting to be supportive he replies: "I can see how my behavior upsets you. Because I want you to be happy, and because I want us to get along, I will try to remember to do what you ask."

Mr. Jones then adds: "Since we are clearing the air, I wish you would stop being mean to me and criticizing me. It makes me feel bad."

Mrs. Jones didn't realize he felt that way. She begins to feel sorry for him. Wanting to please her husband she replies: "I am sorry if I have hurt you, I will try to stop doing that."

In the above example, Mr. and Mrs. Jones behave like Zen masters. Their complaints do not threaten one another. Their *Protector*s are asleep. They consider what their partner is upset about, not themselves.

Unfortunately, if there is any degree of threat within the marital bubble, our *Protector*s will not be asleep. They will be on guard. When *Protector* is present, our automatic response is to first consider feedback from our spouses with regard to ourselves. We unconsciously ask, "What does this action by my partner mean about me?" "Does it mean I am bad? "Does it mean I am unloved?" "Does it mean I am being disrespected?" If the answer is "yes," *Protector* takes over.

Since *Protector* does exist, extricating yourself from TRAP sequences is quite difficult. It is better to avoid them altogether.

Was *Protector* Doing Its Job?

Consider *Protector* in the following situation: The therapists sat in a group supervision meeting. A woman therapist wondered if others had seen the same syndrome in married men that she had observed. She had seen the following:

The men entered into the marriage in a highly enthusiastic state. After a while they began to demonstrate frustration and anger. They showed evidence of mood swings—one minute they were happy, the next minute they were irritable. As the marriage continued they became more withdrawn. They spent more time at work or became overly involved in a hobby.

Sometimes they drank too much, although they could not be described as alcoholic. They did not respond well to anti-depressant medication. Eventually, they left their wives for no apparent reason. This woman said that she had seen this syndrome in all three of her former husbands. "Has anyone else observed it?" she wondered.

This woman's *Protector* had been of no help during her marriages. *Protector* kept her from facing her own threatening behaviors, which were her jealousy, her possessiveness, and her coerciveness. Her behavior had contributed to many escalating TRAP sequences. Eventually her husbands had sought escape.

Although *Protector* had been of no help during marriage, *Protector* was a great help in divorce. Her *Protector* shielded her from the pain of facing her own contribution to her failed marriages.

Protector at its Worst

Mr. Kennedy was scheduled for surgery. Without the surgery he faced the possibility of paralysis. His surgeon was concerned about performing the surgery because Mr. Kennedy seemed to be highly agitated. The doctor feared that his agitation would interfere with recovery, when he was expected to remain immobile for many weeks. The doctor insisted that Mr. Kennedy consult with a psychiatrist prior to the surgery. Mr. Kennedy was enraged. He felt insulted that the doctor believed that he had psychological problems. Acknowledging his problems was more than he could bear. His *Protector* could not allow it. Mr. Kennedy refused to see a psychiatrist. The surgeon postponed the surgery. Mr. Kennedy ended up paralyzed.

Assessing Your Own *Protector*

Understanding the role of your own *Protector* is crucial to avoiding TRAP sequences. In the hypothetical examples below you have done something to hurt your partner's feelings. You find yourself accused of having done something "bad." Consider how your *Protector* might cause you to respond.

1. Your spouse asked you for help with a task. You didn't get around to providing it. In an annoyed voice your spouse says, "I asked you to do this one thing for me and you didn't do it!" Suddenly you feel you have done something wrong. Your self-esteem is threatened. You feel defensive. What would your *Protector* encourage you to do?

     a. Tell your partner that you help a lot more than he/she thinks.

     b. Tell your spouse that he/she isn't that helpful either.

     c. Accuse your spouse of making a big deal out of nothing.

     d. Tell your spouse you would have done it if he/she didn't nag so much.

     e. Think about why you didn't help.

     f. Apologize for not helping.

2. You go to a party. When the party is over your partner is angry at you. He/she thinks you were flirting with someone. You suddenly feel you have done something wrong. Your self-esteem is threatened. You feel defensive. What would your *Protector* encourage you to do?

     a. Deny that you were flirting.

     b. Tell your spouse that he/she is imagining things.

     c. Accuse your spouse of drinking too much.

     d. Say it was just harmless flirting.

     e. Think about whether it upset your partner.

     f. Tell your spouse you will stop if it bothers him/her.

3. Your spouse is trying to tell you something important about his/her day. Your spouse thinks you are not listening and gets angry. You suddenly feel you have done something wrong. Your self-esteem is threatened. You feel defensive. What would your *Protector* encourage you to do?

     a. Deny it. Tell your spouse that you were listening.

     b. Raise your eyebrows, sigh, and say, "Not this again."

    c. Complain that your spouse talks too much.

    d. Tell your spouse that he/she is boring.

    e. Think about why you got distracted.

    f. Say you will try harder to be attentive.

4. You get frustrated with your spouse and raise your voice. Your spouse says he/she doesn't like it when you raise your voice. You suddenly feel you have done something wrong. Your self-esteem is threatened. You feel defensive. What would your *Protector* encourage you to do?

    a. Deny that you are raising your voice.

    b. Blame your spouse for making you mad.

    c. Tell your spouse to shut up.

    d. Claim that your partner would do the same thing.

    e. Think about what you are angry about and apologize.

    f. Tell yourself to control your anger.

5. You get distracted and leave the stove on. In an irritated voice your partner says, "You left the stove on. Why did you do that?" You suddenly feel you have done something wrong. Your self-esteem is threatened. You feel defensive. What would your *Protector* encourage you to do?

    a. Say it is no big deal, nothing happened.

    b. Say someone else left it on.

    c. Point out that your partner also forgets things.

    d. Accuse your partner of being too critical.

    e. Think about how you got distracted and forgot.

    f. Apologize for your mistake.

6. Your partner is annoyed with you for spending money on something that he/she thinks is frivolous. Your partner says, "How could you have wasted money like that?" You suddenly feel that you have done something wrong. Your self-esteem is threatened. You feel defensive. What would your *Protector* encourage you to do?

    a. Claim that it was money well spent

    b. Accuse your partner of trying to control you.

    c. Accuse your partner of wasting more money than you do.

    d. Ignore your partner and watch T.V.

    e. Think about why you made the purchase.

    f.   Say it was wrong and that you will return it.

7. You and your partner agree to watch a video together. You get preoccupied with something else and don't show up to watch it. Your partner gets angry and says she can't count on you. You suddenly feel you have done something wrong. Your self-esteem is threatened. You feel defensive. What would your *Protector* encourage you to do?

    a.   Claim you hadn't agreed on when to watch it.

    b.   Say he/she wasn't there either.

    c.   Say your spouse always tries to ruin things.

    d.   Accuse your partner of being a hypocrite since he/she is always late.

    e.   Say you are sorry.

    f.   Think about why you were not there.

8. After discussing a disagreement with your spouse, he/she complains that you are being overly controlling. You suddenly feel that you have done something wrong. Your self-esteem is threatened. You feel defensive. What would your *Protector* encourage you to do?

    a.   Tell your partner that intent was not to control or criticize.

    b.   Accuse her of being more controlling than you are.

    c.   Storm off.

    d.   Tell your partner to "go to hell."

    e.   Think about how you might be coming across as controlling.

    f.   Apologize and say that "I don't mean to come across this way."

9. Your spouse complains that you left your clothes all over the bedroom again. Your spouse says, "How many times do I have to ask you to pick them up?" You feel you have done something wrong. Your self-esteem is threatened. You feel defensive. What would your *Protector* encourage you to do?

    a.   Say that it isn't that messy.

    b.   Tell him/her to stop being so picky.

    c.   Tell him/her that it isn't healthy to be so anal.

    d.   Ignore the comment.

    e.   Agree that it is a mess.

    f.   Thank your partner for pointing it out.

In the above examples, if you had not flirted, had been a better listener, had cleaned up the bedroom etc. the unpleasant situation could have been avoided. The point of this book is to recognize the consequences of your behavior and avoid behaviors that cause arguments. However, in these examples, that did not happen. Instead, you were accused of being "bad" and you felt defensive, thus involving your *Protector*. If you answered the questions honestly, you will see that in most cases you reacted with some variation of responses a, b, c, or d. If you are exceptionally mature, despite feeling defensive, you could rise above your *Protector* and respond with some variety of responses "e" and "f". Unfortunately, most of us are not that mature.

Don't Go Down that Road: Keeping *Protector* at Bay

Protector is strong. When we feel threatened, *Protector* **will** take over and a TRAP sequence **will** occur. Our best chance to avoid arguments is to recognize situations which will awaken *Protector*. The first step in getting *Protector* under control is to recognize when threat could emerge and avoid going down that road.

Exercise 1: Consider Examples from Your Own Marriage

Imagine your partner complaining about aspects of your married life. Consider how you would respond.

Household Chores

Think about how you handle your household chores. What would your partner complain about? Answer the following:

1. My partner complains that I don't do my household chores. This is what my partner would say:

_____

_____

I would respond:

_____

_____

Is *Protector* involved in my response? _____.

In-laws

Think about how you interact with your partner's family. What would your partner complain about? Answer the following:

My partner complains that I ignore his/her parents. My partner would say:

_____

_____

I would respond:

_____

_____

Is *Protector* involved in my response? _____

Money

Think about how you deal with money. What would your partner complain about? Answer the following:

My partner complains that I waste money. My partner would say:

_____

_____

I would respond:

_____

_____

Is *Protector* involved in my response? _____

The Most Argumentative Situation

Think about the most argumentative situation in your marriage. What would you partner complain about? Answer the following:

My partner would say:

_____

_____

I would respond:

_____

_____

Is *Protector* involved in my response? _____

3	**TRAP Sequences Gone Wild:** **The Road to Divorce**

Fig. 3-1: Trapper Controls the Couple

When TRAP sequences occur too often, spouses become fixed in their threatened/defensive postures. In the presence of the partner they immediately become apprehensive. They are always looking for threat to defend against—and always finding it. Eventually the fighting wears them down. They lose their resilience. They lose the ability to control themselves and become more impulsive. What they say and do becomes more and more hostile and destructive. They are no longer in control of the marriage. The TRAP sequences are now in control of them. Consider Virginia and Mack's marriage.

Virginia and Mack's Marriage

The Romantic Stage

Virginia and Mack met in a divorce support group at their church in rural New England. They were emotional, high drama people. Almost immediately their relationship was passionate. Their time together was devoted solely to each other and it was romantic! Virginia felt that Mack treated her in a way that she had never experienced before. She was euphoric. Her family had never seen her happier. It was the same for Mack.

After Marriage

After marriage everything changed. It appeared to Virginia that Mack was actually far more withdrawn than she had imaged! In addition, Virginia suddenly had to compete for Mack's attention. His job, his kids, and his hunting and fishing all became threats. They drew his attention away from her. When ignored by Mack, Virginia felt inadequate, as though she wasn't good enough to be given attention. The situation activated the many moments of emotional pain contained in her past. *Protector* would not allow this.

With *Protector* in control, Virginia's defensive reaction was to attack Mack's character. She said "You aren't committed; you deceived me; you aren't honest." The problem became Mack's fault, not Virginia's. *Protector* was not dealing with the reality of cause and effect. Accusing him wasn't going to make him more committed; it was only going to make him more defensive. A TRAP sequence was inevitable.

Mack thought of himself as a good and responsible person. When criticized, he experienced a momentary sense of inadequacy and shame. He had his own history of painful emotional moments. His *Protector* quickly helped him engage in a defensive counter-response. Mack angrily denied her accusations and made a counter-accusation. He said that he had no idea how insecure she was. Virginia defended herself again. With both feeling threatened, the TRAP sequences became wilder. Over the months their relationship began to deteriorate.

The Pivotal Event

The pivotal incident occurred after many months of TRAP sequences. Mack had been reading a fishing magazine after dinner. Virginia felt that he was avoiding her, and this wakened her *Protector*. She angrily complained that he was hiding behind his magazine. Mack felt annoyed, but he suppressed his anger and ignored her, thus fueling her sense of rejection. Her defensive reaction was to claim that he wasn't the man he had portrayed himself to be. This criticism stung Mack. It elicited that shameful/painful sense of inadequacy.

His *Protector* was now awake. Another TRAP sequence ensued. Mack was a dramatic man. In anger, he threw off his wedding ring. He stormed out of the house and got in his truck. To Virginia this meant that he was leaving the marriage. She panicked. Knowing that she had to prevent the marriage from ending, she ran after him. Seeing her approach, he gunned the engine. As Mack's truck moved down the driveway, Virginia reached the passenger door, grabbed for the handle and fell. Mack slammed on the brakes. Both were stunned. What was happening to them?

Despite their distress over the incident, other high drama TRAP sequences followed. They escalated to a new and dangerous level. Mack and Virginia passed the point of no return. The level of threat had become too high and neither could tolerate it. They filed for divorce. Both were regretful. However, with their fight or flight systems constantly elevated, the relationship had become a danger to their physical and emotional well being. The TRAP sequences had beaten them down.

A Silent TRAP Leads To Divorce: Miles and Jill

Protector does not always initiate attack and high drama as a means of defense. In order to shield spouses from pain, *Protector* also initiates silent withdrawal. This also leads to TRAP sequences. Consider Miles and Jill. Throughout their lives both Miles and Jill had been frightened by anger and had withdrawn from it. When someone else was angry, they immediately felt that it was their fault.

Miles and Jill met when they shared the same piano teacher at a music seminary in the Midwest. It turned out that neither continued with music, but they did continue with each other.

Once they married, fear of the other's anger became the predominant theme in their relationship. Both were careful around the other. Neither would raise his/her voice, use derogatory language, nor make demands of the other. Anticipating a possible negative reaction, they would rarely complain or offer strong opinions. Although they experienced the inevitable clash of spousal needs, they were never able to develop ways of expressing their needs and dealing with their differences. Unlike Mack and Virginia, who had too little impulse control, Miles and Jill had too much.

Their Inevitable Clashes: Miles' Mother

One of the early problems in their marriage was Miles's overbearing mother. Jill was intimidated by her. So was Miles. On the few occasions when Jill found the courage to complain about his mother, Miles felt threatened. Her complaints implied he should confront his mother. In his family no one confronted his mother. He resented the implied pressure on him to speak up. When he did nothing Jill felt betrayed and withdrew. Miles reacted to her withdrawal by withdrawing himself, resulting in a silent TRAP sequence.

As time went on, when they visited his mother, Jill learned to keep her resentment inside. Jill wanted Miles to notice that she was uncomfortable. Miles could have said, "Is something bothering you?" But inquiring would mean exposing himself to her resentment. Instead, he retreated into himself. Visits to his family were dominated by this unspoken TRAP sequence. Their trips home afterwards were tense.

Their Inevitable Clashes: Miles' Poor Listening

The flow of information between Jill and Miles had always been meager. Miles didn't have a lot to say. However, initially he seemed willing to listen. Jill would ramble on about this and that. As time went on Miles began to feel suffocated by Jill's ramblings. She never seemed to get to the point. He began showing signs of disinterest. He would look at his watch, pick up the newspaper, or turn on the T.V. This hurt Jill. She began to feel that she was uninteresting. *Protector* took over and she retreated. When Miles saw her retreat, he retreated. This silent TRAP sequence cut down still further on the flow of communication between them.

Their Inevitable Clashes: Jill's Poor Listening

Miles had his own grievances. Although he offered very little in the way of conversation, he was angry at Jill for not showing more interest in him. On the few occasions when he took the risk and shared his inner experience, he found the results hurtful. Jill was often judgmental about his world view. She also didn't remember the details when he discussed his photography or his professional interests. Once burned, twice shy. Miles stopped sharing and retreated. Then Jill retreated.

Their Inevitable Clashes: Their Daughter—Debbie

Miles and Jill probably could have survived these TRAP sequences. However, it was their adopted daughter, Debbie, who generated the most threat. Debbie's temperament was unlike either of them. Debbie's learning difficulties made school difficult. Her impulsivity made keeping friends difficult. In her teenage and young adult years Debbie's life was about boys, drugs and rock & roll. Counselors and rehab centers followed.

During Debbie's adolescence, Miles felt that Jill over-indulged her. As a result, he believed Debbie lacked self-discipline. Although Miles was a silent man, he did speak up about this. However, he did so in an angry tone that paralyzed his wife emotionally. When she heard his anger, she went into shut down mode. This infuriated Miles. Miles could not get his wife to listen to him. Eventually, he gave up.

Miles's frustration mounted until he refused to speak to Jill at all. The TRAP sequences gained increasing power over the couple. Miles began bringing crossword puzzles to the dinner table. Then he stopped coming to dinner altogether.

Miles was angry at Jill. Jill was angry at Jack. For two anger-sensitive individuals the situation became intolerable. Emotional detachment was their solution. Both spent long hours at work. When not at work, Miles retreated to photography. Jill involved herself in church activities. After a year of painful silence, Jill could tolerate no more. She knew she had to leave the marriage. Both regretted their divorce, but neither seemed able to prevent it. The silent TRAP sequence had overpowered them.

Jill and Miles were nothing like Mack and Virginia. Yet, they had one thing in common: TRAP sequences took over and destroyed their marriages. In the next chapter we will examine more closely the threatening behaviors that bring on the destructive TRAP sequence.

4	# How We Threaten Our Partner and Become the Enemy

Fig. 4-1: How We Threaten Our Partner

Threatening behaviors have many sources. They come from the frustration and anger that spouses feel during the clash of needs. They come from *Protector*'s need to defend against painful feelings and its tendency to find threat where it doesn't exist. They come from our own insecurities, our feelings of inferiority and fears of abandonment. They also come from aspects of our personality we aren't even aware of, our biologically based temperament characteristics. Through sheer luck some of us inherit calm, non-reactive personalities that are conducive to successful marriage. Others of us are not so fortunate.

What Are *You* Like To Live With?

What are you like to live with? How many threatening signals do you send out? Would someone interacting with you feel accepted, relaxed, bullied, ignored, bored, or suspicious? *Protector* doesn't want you to know what your impact is on others, but you need to know. Your marriage might depend upon it. The process of repairing your marriage begins by understanding which of your behaviors fill the marital bubble with threat. Below we describe some typical threatening spousal behaviors.

Lack of Support, Disregard, Selfishness

Typical behavior

To be supportive means to be responsive to what is important to your partner. With regard to support, it is what spouses do *not* do that becomes threatening. This occurs when a partner is counting on help, attention, or affection and repeatedly doesn't get it. The clothes don't get picked up; there is no help with the kids; the spouse doesn't listen; or in a moment of crisis the partner isn't there.

Sometimes spouses are not supportive during a clash of spousal needs because *they want what they want when they want it*. But in other instances this is not the case. The needs of one spouse are relatively mild compared to the other, yet the less needy spouse remains unresponsive to the partner. Let's consider some reasons why.

Selfishness

Sometimes, being supportive feels like too much trouble. We know what our partners want. We could respond, but we just don't. It feels to us as though it is too much trouble to be responsive. Perhaps we think we are too tired. Perhaps we are too lazy. Perhaps we are too worried and preoccupied. We could make the effort, but we do not.

This is selfishness. Many TRAP sequence begin because of unnecessary acts of selfishness.

Egocentricity

Egocentricity is not selfishness. Selfish acts occur when we understand what our partners want and don't respond. Egocentricity is different. Egocentricity occurs because we are each prisoners of our own experience. Because our partner's life experience is so different from ours, it is difficult for us to comprehend what our partners may be thinking or feeling. As a result, we often do not grasp what is important to them.

On other occasions we do grasp our partner's needs, but quickly lose our grasp because nothing in our own experience helps us maintain our understanding. If something is not important to us, it is hard to understand why it is important to them. The result is that we easily disregard what we don't intuitively understand.

If our partners are equally egocentric, it becomes difficult for them to recognize that we don't understand. Egocentricity makes life in the marriage bubble difficult. It leads to feelings of intentional disregard, when in fact there have been none.

Fear of Being Controlled

If being supportive means that we feel controlled, then we may not do it. If taking out the garbage, or being home on time, or helping our spouse, feels like bending to the will of another, we might resist. Feeling controlled may feel demeaning. It becomes a huge contributor to lack of support.

Perceiving the Partner as the Enemy

When threat and TRAP sequences are present, no support will be forthcoming. No one is going to support the enemy.

Your Partner's Emotional Reaction to Lack of Support

Is your partner sensitive to being disregarded? Of course! What does it feel like to be on the receiving end of disregard? It elicits a complex set of painful emotions: feelings of being unworthy; feelings of being unimportant; feelings of being unloved. Disregard in marriage activates earlier experiences of disregard at the hands of significant others. These memories are painful and *Protector* will instantly defend against them. The result will be a TRAP sequence.

Think about Yourself! How much threat do you create in the marriage bubble through lack of support?

Exercise 2: Does Lack Of Support Lead
To a TRAP Pattern In Your Relationship?

Your Spouse is not Supportive

Step 1: You are worried about a work proposal due on Friday. You ask your partner to check the document for errors. Your partner doesn't do it.

What would your reaction be? What would you say?

_____

_____

Would your response be threatening to your partner?

_____

_____

How would your partner react to what you would say?

_____

_____

Would the interaction escalate into an argument? _____.

You are not Supportive of Your Partner

Step 1: Your partner is worried about getting to work on time. He/she asks to take the first shower. You forget and get in the shower, thereby making your partner still later.

How do you imagine your partner would react? What would your partner say?

_____

_____

Would this be threatening to you?

_____

_____

How do you imagine you would you react to what your partner would said?

_____

_____

Would the interaction escalate into an argument? _____.

Criticism and Derogation

Typical Critical Behavior

Critical spouses have a difficult time in marriage. Without being aware of it, they cloud the bubble with threat and create defensiveness in their partners. The typical behavior of a critical spouse is as follows:

- You shouldn't do ... (You are behaving badly);
- I can't believe you said that... (It was wrong);
- It would be better if you did... (My way is better);
- Why didn't you do... (You are incompetent, lazy);
- What is wrong with you? You are so... (You are mean, selfish).

Why are people critical?

Often spouses observe something that needs to be corrected. But spouses who are critical rarely offer the critical observation constructively—in a spirit of concern or kindness. Instead, it is often delivered when the spouse is frustrated and attempting to be "one-up." Your *Protector* loves criticism because it puts you in the superior position. For that moment, the criticizing spouse feels free from whatever incompetence, laziness, selfishness, etc. is implied. This is a self-deception, but it feels good at the moment.

Typical Derogatory Behavior

Derogatory behavior is criticism on steroids. What angry spouses say to one another when frustrated and in the middle of a TRAP sequence can be brutal. The words listed below are examples. They are offensive. But be honest with yourself. Have you ever used terms like this when angry with your spouse? In the real world, these are words people use when angry. They are intended to hurt and they do:

idiot	whore
stupid	fucker
crazy	bastard
sick	scumbag
loser	slob
asshole	pig
bitch	

The list is endless. Actually it can become far worse.

When spouses realize what they have said, they often feel remorseful. Unfortunately, in the heat of a battle, they lose control and the damage is done. The partner does not forget what has been said. The wound does not heal quickly. Hopefully, seeing these words in print will help spouses think twice. There is no faster way to destroy the quality of the marriage than through derogation.

Your Partner's Emotional Response to Criticism/Derogation

Is your partner sensitive to criticism and derogation? The answer, of course, is yes! Criticism elicits feelings of worthlessness. Our self-esteem is threatened. When we are criticized our emotional brains are activated. Our entire history of feeling demeaned or shamed by others is resurrected. As we know, *Protector* will not permit emotional pain to persist. In the bubble, the criticizer will be *identified as the enemy* and will soon be on the receiving end of a hurtful counter-reaction. *Protector* insists on it.

Think about yourself! How often are you critical or derogatory?

Exercise 3: Does Criticism Lead to a
TRAP Pattern In Your Relationship?

Your Spouse Criticizes You

Step 1: Your spouse says you are an idiot and don't know what you are talking about. What do you imagine your reaction would be? What would you say?

_____

_____

Would your reaction be threatening to your partner? _____

What do you imagine your spouse's reaction would be? What would your partner say?

_____

_____

Would the interaction escalate into an argument?_____

You Criticize Your Partner

Step 1: You say to your partner that he/she is an idiot and doesn't know what he/she is talking about.

What do you imagine your spouse's reaction would be? What would your spouse say?

_____

_____

What do you imagine your reaction would be to your partner? What would you say?

_____

_____

Would the interaction escalate into an argument? _____

Control, Coercion, and Dominance

Typical Controlling Behavior

Controlling people have a difficult time in marriage. During the clash of needs these spouses often become coercive in order to get what they want. They find ways to intimidate and prevail. Sometimes they insinuate that there will be negative consequences if they do not get their way (no affection, no sex, or no financial support). Sometimes they nag, complain, or pout until they get what they want. Coercion involves a one-way relationship. The coercer implies: "My needs are more important than yours. I will force you to meet them." This behavior is threatening and will eventually result in the partner perceiving the spouse as the enemy.

Why are people coercive?

It is in some people's nature to dominate. By nature they are outspoken, tend to take the initiative and are decisive. However, even those who are not naturally assertive like to be in control. Our world seems safer and more predictable when we are in control. What domineering spouses fail to understand is that their partners will not accept their unspoken definition of the marriage as a relationship between a boss and a subordinate or instructor and a student. Some marriages start out that way, but few remain that way.

Your Partner's Emotional Reaction to Feeling Controlled

Is your partner sensitive to being controlled? The answer is yes! The partner who begins to feel less than equal in the relationship will begin to feel smothered, an obvious breeding ground for threat and TRAP sequences. Most of us dislike being controlled. Some fear it to the extent that we organize our lives around avoiding it. Spouses on the receiving end of coercion feel resentful, restricted, and helpless. The resentment and anger fills the bubble with threat.

Think about yourself! How much threat do you put into the bubble by being domineering?

Exercise 4: Does Control Lead To A TRAP Pattern In Your Relationship?

Your Partner is Controlling

Step 1: You and your partner are painting the front porch together. You are scraping paint from a window. Your partner comes over and tells you about a better way to do it. You tell your partner that you prefer your own way. Five minutes later your partner comes over and again tells you how you should be doing it.

What do you imagine your reaction would be? What would you say?

_____

_____

_____

Would your reaction be threatening to your partner?

_____

_____

What do you imagine your partner would say?

_____

_____

_____

Would the interaction escalate into an argument?_____.

You are Controlling

Step 1: You and your partner are discussing where to go for dinner. You suggest a Chinese restaurant. Your partner says he/she is tired of Chinese food. Your partner suggests an Italian restaurant. You say "no." Your partner suggests a Mexican restaurant. You say "no" again. Your partner makes another suggestion and you say "no." Then you say, "We either go Chinese or I am not going."

How do you imagine your partner would react? What would your partner say?

_____

_____

_____

Would what your partner said be threatening to you?

_____

_____

How do you imagine would you react? What would you do?

_____

_____

Would the interaction escalate into an argument?_____.

Withdrawal and Avoidance

The Typical Behavior of Withdrawers

Marriage is not easy for withdrawers. Withdrawers are quick to avoid conflict. Withdrawers may physically vacate the premises. More often they become silent or evasive. They tune out mentally and shut down emotionally. They automatically withdraw in order to avoid a situation in which their partner will become upset or angry. Unfortunately for them, their withdrawal upsets the partner.

Why are People Withdrawers?

Withdrawal is a classic means of self-protection. Withdrawers fear potential conflict. Some fear the possibility of being abandoned. The mere hint of anger causes withdrawers to disengage.

The problem is, you can run, but you can't hide in the marital bubble. When one spouse tries to withdraw, the message the partner receives is, "You don't want to communicate with me"; "You are not interested in me"; or worst of all "You are abandoning me." Thus, the issue of abandonment is raised for both parties.

Often, withdrawal prompts the rejected spouse to pursue the withdrawing partner. What occurs is a pattern of pursue/withdraw. One spouse constantly seeks engagement. This drives the partner further away, which prompts still greater pursuit in an endless vicious cycle.

In some marriages both spouses are withdrawers. In this case neither pursues the other. Both withdraw and get the isolation from conflict they seek. However, neither will be satisfied with this. It only makes them lonely.

Withdrawal and Your Partner's Emotional Reaction

Is your partner sensitive to being avoided? Yes! What does it feel like to be on the receiving end of withdrawal? It feels lonely. It is depressing. We are social animals. Without connection to our partner, the marriage feels meaningless. Withdrawal will inevitably lead to threat. Withdrawers need to learn to tolerate some degree of conflict, since the clash of spousal needs is inevitable.

Think About Yourself! How much threat do you put into the bubble by engaging in avoidance and withdrawal?

Exercise 5: Does Withdrawal Lead to
a TRAP Pattern In Your Relationship?

Your Partner Withdraws

Step 1: You and your partner go for a walk together. Your partner is walking too fast. In an annoyed voice you say, "Slow down." Your partner says nothing and emotionally withdraws.

How do you imagine you would you react? What would you do?

_____

_____

Would what you do be threatening to your partner?

_____

_____

How do you imagine your partner would react to what you did?

_____

_____

Would the interaction escalate into a period of cold silence?_____.

You Withdraw

Step 1: Your partner tries to give you a hug and you withdraw.
How do you imagine your partner would react? What would your partner do?

_____

_____

Would what your partner did be threatening to you?

_____

_____

How do you imagine you would react?

_____

_____

Would the interaction escalate into a period of cold silence_____?

Anger and Angry Outbursts

Typical Angry Behavior

Angry, impulsive people have a difficult time in marriage. When frustrated they raise their voices, they yell, they hurl insults, they destroy property, they become physically intimidating and fill the bubble with threat. This obviously will elicit TRAP sequences.

Sometimes the anger we feel as spouses is justified. It is a frustrated reaction to our partner's unhelpful behavior. Despite this, when we lose control of our anger, it becomes our problem. Nothing justifies the impulsive lashing out that can follow the experience of anger.

Why Are People Angry?

Feeling Normal Frustration. Anger is a normal response to frustration. From an evolutionary perspective anger helped our ancestors become mobilized to overcome difficult obstacles. Anger may still help us in this way. If we fail at a task and become angry, the anger may help us become more determined to succeed. However, in the marital bubble anger does not help. It only makes things worse.

Experiencing Intentional Disregard. Anger occurs when we misinterpret our partner's behavior as intentionally hurtful. Our spouses may do many things that frustrate us, but usually, they are not trying to hurt or punish us. They are simply acting on their own needs. We think their behavior is directed toward us, when it is not.

Whether our anger is realistic or based on misinterpretation, if we cannot manage it effectively, we will fill the marital bubble fill with threat.

Your Own Anger and Your Partner's Emotional Reaction

What does it feel like to be on the receiving end of anger? Few people can remain neutral in the face of anger. Our emotional brains are wired to experience anger as a threat. People respond to anger with emotions ranging from mild discomfort, to fear, to total emotional paralysis. The angry spouse becomes the enemy—someone who must be defended against.

Think About Yourself! How much anger do you put into the marital bubble?

Exercise 6: Does Anger Lead to A TRAP Pattern in Your Relationship?

Your Partner is Angry

Step 1: You and your partner are having a difference of opinion. A look of anger crosses your partner's face. He/she begins to glare and gets in your face. Your partner's voice becomes loud and harsh.

What do you imagine your reaction would be? What would you do?

_____

_____

Would your reaction threaten your partner?

_____

_____

How do you imagine your partner would react to what you did?

_____

_____

What would your partner do?

_____

_____

Would the interaction escalate into an argument?_____.

You are Angry

Step 1: You and your partner are having a difference of opinion. A look of anger crosses your face. You begin to glare and get in your partner's face. Your voice becomes loud and harsh.

What do you imagine your partner's reaction would be? What would your partner do?

_____

_____

Would your partner's reaction threaten you?

_____

_____

What do you imagine your reaction would be to what your partner did?

_____

_____

Would the interaction escalate into an argument?_____

Insecurity and Jealousy

Typical Jealous Behavior

Jealous people have a difficult time in marriage. Jealousy-prone spouses feel threatened if the partner appears too interested in another person or activity. The insecure reaction is, "You must prefer that other person or activity to me." The feeling of being non-preferred is accompanied by anger and an accusation: "You are not attracted to me; you don't care about me; you don't love me!" In order to feel secure, the spouse will try to prevent the partner from engaging with the threatening person or the activity.

Jealous people tend to see the world in terms of friends and enemies. The mindset is: Whom are you for and whom are you against? If you are on my team you can't be on that other team. If you like me, then you must dislike him/her.

This kind of thinking can plague both the jealous spouse and the partner. The jealous spouse becomes threatened by the partner's attention to work and desire for success; the partner's interest in family or friends; or even attractive men or women who pass on the street.

Why Are People Jealous?

From an evolutionary perspective jealousy may have been useful in identifying sexual rivals and warding them off. Thus, jealousy may have helped insure that one kept his/her mate. It also helped the offspring survive. All of us are wired to be jealous on occasion.

Unfortunately, some of us are prone to more extreme jealousy. In our families of origin we may have experienced neglect and deprivation. As a result we are attention and affection hungry. Once married, we have an unarticulated hope that the partner can fill the emotional void derived from childhood. The partner's loving behavior may fill the emptiness to some degree. When the partner's attention is elsewhere the emotional void returns.

These spouses become their own worst enemies. Within the marital bubble, any small failure by the partner to be attentive or affectionate will trigger a painful sense of deprivation. This jealousy can fill the marital bubble with threat.

Jealousy and Your Partner's Emotional Reaction

The partner of a jealous spouse feels under chronic attack. His/her every move is scrutinized and viewed with suspicion. The intent behind every behavior is questioned. The constant question becomes, "Do you prefer someone else, or something else, to me?" This burdens and restricts the scrutinized spouse, who feels increasingly claustrophobic. In self-protection, the partner begins to hide innocuous daily experiences in order to ward off more suspicious questioning. This secrecy makes the jealous spouse more insecure, thus intensifying threat within the bubble.

Think About Yourself! How much threat do you put into the bubble by being jealous?

Exercise 7: Does Jealousy Lead To A TRAP Pattern In Your Relationship?

Your Partner is Jealous

Step 1: You and your partner were at a party. After the party your partner says that you spent too much time talking to an attractive member of the opposite sex. Your partner says that it was obvious that the two of you were flirting.

What do you imagine that your reaction be? What would you say?

_____

_____

Would you reaction threaten your partner?

_____

_____

How do you imagine that your partner would you react to what you said?

_____

_____

Would the interaction escalate into an argument?_____.

You Are Jealous

Step 1: Your partner continues to exchange email messages with an old fiancé. You don't like this and tell your partner so.

What do you imagine that your partner's reaction would be? What would your partner say?

_____

_____

Would your partner's reaction threaten you?

_____

_____

How do you imagine you would respond to what your partner said?

_____

_____

Would the interaction escalate into an argument?_____.

Lying, Secrets, and Irresponsibility

Typical Secretive Behavior

Secretive people have a difficult time in marriage. They don't share their inner experience with their partners, thus creating an information vacuum. This becomes fertile ground for suspiciousness. Lying is even more troublesome. Spouses will lie about whom they have been with and what they have done. If what they have done is irresponsible the situation becomes more destructive. They may have abused drugs, had affairs, wasted money, or otherwise engaged in behavior that is reckless.

The thinking becomes, "My partner will not like what I spent money on; whom I have spoken to; what I have been doing; how much I drank, etc. Thus, I will not tell my partner." Inevitably the partner will discover what has been hidden and mistrust will grow. "What else is my partner doing that I don't know about?" the spouse will wonder. The concealing and lying fills the marriage with threat. Unfortunately, for some spouses, lying and secretiveness is a way of life.

Why Do People Lie?

Many people who lie learned early in life that being honest doesn't pay. In their families of origin openly asking for what they wanted or telling others how they felt resulted in unresponsiveness or opposition. Thus, they learned to go underground and get what they wanted be being secretive. They learned not to expect support from others. They carry this implicit assumption into marriage and assume that nothing good will come of sharing their inner experience with the partner. They remain cautious and share little.

Jealous and secretive people seem to find one another and a vicious cycle emerges. Jealousy breeds lying. Lying breeds insecurity and jealousy. A vicious TRAP pattern is the result.

Lying and Your Partner's Emotional Reaction

Is your partner sensitive to being lied to? The answer is yes! What does it feel like to be on the receiving end of lying? It creates uncertainty, mistrust, and anxiety. Is my partner secretly seeing someone else? Is my partner going to leave me? Is my partner spending us into bankruptcy? Is my partner doing drugs or involved in criminal activity?

In the absence of information, the partner's imagination can run wild and create chronic anxiety. The anxious spouse will, in turn, make life miserable for the secretive partner by engaging in threatening accusations.

Think About Yourself! How much threat and mistrust do you put into the bubble by being irresponsible and secretive?

Exercise 8: Does Lying Lead to a
TRAP Pattern In Your Relationship?

You Lie to Your Partner

Step 1: You spent the night out drinking with your friends. You don't want your partner to know about this. When he/she asks where you were, you say you were at work. "That is a lie. I called you at work and you didn't answer," your partner replies.

What do you imagine your reaction would be? What would you say?

_____

_____

Would your reaction threaten your partner?

_____

_____

What do you imagine your partner's reaction to you would be?

_____

_____

Would this threaten you?

_____

_____

Would this interaction escalate into an argument?_____

Your Partner Lies to You

Step 1: You look at the credit card bill and there are big charges you didn't know about. You ask your partner about the charges. Your partner denies making them.

What do you imagine your reaction would be? What would you say?

_____

_____

Would your reaction threaten your partner?

_____

_____

What do you imagine your partner's reaction would be to what you said?

_____

_____

Would this be threatening to you?

_____

_____

Would this interaction escalate into an argument?_____

Assess Your Own Threatening Behaviors

The Challenge: Rating Yourself Honestly

Rate yourself on criticism, lack of support, coercion, lying, jealousy, withdrawal, and anger. Use the five point scale below. The challenge is to honestly evaluate yourself. *Protector* will not like this. If you are high on some dimensions, thus contributing to threat in the bubble, *Protector* will want you to deny it. Don't let *Protector* win.

To rise above *Protector* and be objective, remember this: No one is perfect. You are not a god. You are not a superman. You are not Mother Teresa. You are merely human. Human beings have flaws. Despite your flaws you have self-worth. You are an acceptable human being. If you remind yourself of this, perhaps you can look honestly at how you contribute threat to the marital bubble.

Rate Your Partner

In addition to rating yourself, you must also rate your partner and rely on ratings from your partner. The information you need to improve your marriage is also contained in the feedback you get from your partner. If your partner says that you are overly critical, unsupportive, jealous etc. then you probably are. Even if you disagree, it is your partner's perception of you that is important.

If there is much arguing and tension in your relationship, your ratings and your partner's ratings will probably be subject to exaggeration. Each *Protector* will want to shift all the "bad" qualities onto the other. Don't use this as an excuse to minimize your partner's feedback. Take it seriously. Just be sure you don't fall into the trap of believing that the negative feedback makes you a bad person.

Marital Rating Scales

Rate Your Partner and Yourself on the Following Dimensions

Being unsupportive and disregarding	None	A Little	Moderate Amount	Significant Amount	Severe Amount
You	1	2	3	4	5
Your Partner	1	2	3	4	5

Being critical and derogatory	None	A Little	Moderate Amount	Significant Amount	Severe Amount
You	1	2	3	4	5
Your Partner	1	2	3	4	5

Being controlling and coercive	None	A Little	Moderate Amount	Significant Amount	Severe Amount
You	1	2	3	4	5
Your Partner	1	2	3	4	5

Being withdrawing and avoidant	None	A Little	Moderate Amount	Significant Amount	Severe Amount
You	1	2	3	4	5
Your Partner	1	2	3	4	5

Being angry and impulsive	None	A Little	Moderate Amount	Significant Amount	Severe Amount
You	1	2	3	4	5
Your Partner	1	2	3	4	5

Being jealous and insecure	None	A Little	Moderate Amount	Significant Amount	Severe Amount
You	1	2	3	4	5
Your Partner	1	2	3	4	5

Being secretive and lying	None	A Little	Moderate Amount	Significant Amount	Severe Amount
You	1	2	3	4	5
Your Partner	1	2	3	4	5

Scoring the Marital Rating Scales

For each of the seven threatening behaviors enter your rating of yourself, and your partner's rating of you, in the appropriate box in the table below. Then, add your ratings to your partner's ratings to get a total score for each behavior. Enter the total score in the box labeled "Total." If you are doing the ratings alone, just use your own ratings.

	Unsupportive Disregarding	Critical Derogatory	Controlling Coercive	Withdrawing Avoidant	Angry Impulsive	Jealous Insecure	Lying Secretive
Your Rating of Yourself							
Your Partner's Rating of You							
Total							

	Unsupportive Disregarding	Critical Derogatory	Controlling Coercive	Withdrawing Avoidant	Angry Impulsive	Jealous Insecure	Lying Secretive
Your Rating of Your Partner							
Your Partner's Rating of Self							
Total							

Plot the total score for each threatening behavior on the threat profile below.

What is your most elevated area? This is the area in which you are creating the most threat in the marital bubble. It is the way you are contributing to the TRAP pattern. It is what you need to work on.

Another way to determine what to work on is to have your partner fill out the "What Bothers Me the Most about My Partner" scale. Use these ratings to determine which behaviors you need to work on

Perceived Threat Level

Perceived Threat level	Unsupportive Disregarding	Critical Derogatory	Controlling Coercive	Withdrawing Avoidant	Angry Impulsive	Jealous Insecure	Lying Secretive
10							
9							
8							
7							
6							
5							
4							
3							
2							
1							

What bothers me the most about my partner...

	Bothers me a little	Bothers me a lot	Bothers me the most
My partner's disregard and lack of support	1	2	3
My partner's derogation and criticism	1	2	3
My partner's control and coercion	1	2	3
My partner's withdrawal and avoidance	1	2	3
My partner's anger and impulsivity	1	2	3
My partner's jealousy and insecurity	1	2	3
My partner's lying and secretiveness	1	2	3

Exercise 9: Describe Your Worst TRAP Sequence

Choose the most troubling argument in your marriage. Describe what transpires using the TRAP sequence model.

What Happens At Step 1? What do you perceive to be the threatening behavior? Be specific. What does the spouse do?

What Happens At Step 2? Who reacts defensively to the threatening behavior at Step 1? Be specific. What does the spouse do?

What Happens At Step 3? What is the counter-defensive reaction to the threatening behavior at Step 2? Who reacts counter-defensively? Be specific. What does the spouse do?

Alexander and Sophia Fill out the TRAP Sequence Form

Alexander and Sophia had a repetitive argument when driving in the car. Being a passenger in the car was difficult for Sophia. Alexander's driving made her nervous. When Sophia was nervous she would warn Alexander about oncoming vehicles, about what lane to be in, and about when he was going too fast. She often felt he ignored her concerns.

When Alexander heard her directives he would think, "She has to be in control. She thinks I can't drive." This created a fleeting sense of incompetence and a moment of emotional pain. Protector intervened. Alexander's emotional pain was quickly replaced with anger, disregard, and criticism.

The sequence involved the following steps: (1) Alexander drives fast; (2) Sophia becomes nervous and directs; (3) Alexander feels controlled, dismisses here concerns and criticizes; (4) Sophia defends; (5) Alexander becomes angrier.

Many couples have mild varieties of this argument; however, Alexander and Sophia had taken it to a dangerous level. When the argument escalated, one or the other would get out of the car and walk—occasionally on highways that were dangerous for pedestrians. Following these arguments, they barely spoke to one another.

Below, are Sophia and Alexander's versions of the TRAP sequence.

Sophia's Version of the TRAP Sequence

What Happens At Step 1? What is the threatening behavior? Be Specific.

> *"He yells at me in the car. He doesn't understand why I'm upset and doesn't try to help me."*

From the Sophie's perspective, the sequence begins with yelling and lack of understanding. From her description it would seem that her husband's yelling emerges out of his own angry personality, i.e. not in reaction to her directives. In reality, the husband has reacted badly to feeling controlled. It is hard for her to see her own role in provoking his anger.

What Happens At Step 2? What is the defensive reaction?

"I get upset that he is yelling. I tell him that I am not trying to control him. I just want him to be more aware of my discomfort and to help me."

She denies being controlling. Instead, she accuses him of being unsympathetic.

What Happens At Step 3? What is the counter-defensive-reaction? Be specific.

"He gets mad because I deny that I am trying to control him. 'Why don't you just admit it?' he says."

Sophia describes her husband's angry and dismissive reaction to her threatening behavior. She sees the following TRAP sequence. Step 1— he yells. Step 2—she defends herself. Step 3—he counter-accuses

Alexander's Version of the TRAP Sequence

What Happens At Step 1? What is the threatening behavior at Step 1? Be specific.

"My wife insists on telling me how to drive."

From the husband's perspective Step 1 is his wife's threatening behavior—her bossy directives. He appears to see her behavior as emerging out of her own controlling personality—not as a reaction to his behavior.

What Happens At Step 2? What is the threatening behavior at Step 2? Be specific.

"I feel like I am being told what to do. This makes me mad."

Alexander can acknowledge that he gets angry, but omits that he raises his voice and dismisses her concerns.

What Happens At Step 3? What is the threatening behavior? Be specific?

"My wife denies that she is trying to control me."

Alexander describes how his wife reacts to his behavior. She gets defensive and denies that she is trying to control him. Both see the initial threatening behavior (Step 1) as emerging from a character flaw in the other's personality. The wife sees the trigger as her husband's angry yelling. The husband sees the trigger as the wife's controlling nature. Neither can see that each is influencing the other. If Sophia could see that his yelling is related to her directives and if the Alexander could see that his wife's directives are a reaction to his driving and his ignoring her, both would be better off.

What are they to do? They can't even agree on the steps in the TRAP sequence. Actually, it doesn't matter. The point isn't which came first, the chicken or the egg. The point is to consider this: what can I do to break out of the TRAP sequence?

If they consider both versions of the TRAP sequence, each will know what to do. Alexander must find a way to reassure his wife when driving. Sophia must find a way to avoid the directives that bother her husband. If they consider each other's perception of the TRAP sequence, they will have a guide to work with.

In the next chapter we will consider in greater detail how to change Step 1 threatening behaviors.

5	How to Change Threatening Behaviors at Step #1

Fig. 5-1: The Couple Defeats the Trapper

How do you avoid your own threatening behaviors and subsequent TRAP sequences? What do you have to do to become more supportive, less critical, or less coercive? Below we discuss how you change your behavior. You begin the process of change by becoming more aware of what is happening in your interaction with your spouse.

Awareness of Interactions: The Task and the Relationship

Often, when you are with your partner, there are two things going on simultaneously: the task and the relationship. Many spouses spend far too much time thinking about what they are doing (the task)and far too little time thinking about how they are behaving with their partners as they do it (the relationship).

Consider the following challenging situation for a newly married couple—they decide to wallpaper the bathroom together. Many spouses approach this as though there is only one goal: getting the wallpaper right. Actually there are two goals. The second goal is to complete the job and still like one another when it is over.

Accomplishing the second goal is not easy since wallpapering is frustrating. It is fertile ground for criticism, anger, and withdrawal. If spouses focus solely on the wallpapering, and ignore the relationship, they may end up with an attractive bathroom; however, they may also end up hating one another. If this happens it is because they failed to focus on the second task. They failed to maintain an awareness of how their own behavior affects the partner.

It might be wise to think of marriage as a series of situations like wallpapering. As you engage in these tasks, you must scan the interaction and ask yourself, "How am I behaving? How is it going between the two of us?"

Think about the Specific Threatening Behavior

Think specifically about the threatening behavior that you were rated highest on. Think about the people in your life: your parents, your friends, your work colleagues. Which of them are high on the same characteristic? How do you feel about them? Are you comfortable with them when they act out this characteristic? Look at other marriages. What do you see going on in these marriages when one of them behaves this way?

Monitor Yourself for the Relevant Behavior

Once you have begun to focus on the relationship, you need to monitor your behavior for relevant threatening behavior. As you interact with your partner, ask yourself, "Am I being controlling? Am I withdrawing? Am I getting angry? Am I forgetting about my partner and focusing on myself? Am I being lazy? Can I summon the energy to do what needs to be done for my partner?"

Notice what happens in your interactions when you engage in this behavior. Notice what happens when you do not. When the behavior in question is present, does it lead to a TRAP sequence?

Recognize The Choice Point And Ask: What Will The Consequences Of My Behavior Be?

As you interact with your partner there will be many choice points. You must recognize when you have reached a choice point. At the choice point you can give in to the impulse to be coercive, or to be derogatory, or to withdraw. Or you can decide to control that impulse. If you have been monitoring your behavior and are prepared for the choice point, then you will be able make the right choice. Control of your behavior comes from preparation. It comes from awareness of your behavior and recognition of the choice point.

At the choice point, when you have the impulse to engage in the threatening behavior, you must ask yourself, **"What will be the consequence of my doing this?"** If I forget to call home after I promised to, what will happen? If I lie about what I spent money on, what will happen? If I criticize, what will happen? Will I end up in an argument? Do I want to deal with that? I can go down that road. I have been down it before and know what it is like. Or I can call home, or not spend the money, or not criticize and avoid the argument. **It is my choice. It is up to me.**

Spouses who have some success in choosing to avoid the threatening behavior will begin to notice a change. There will be less arguing. There will be less tension. They will see that their awareness and monitoring has begun to pay off. But there is still a long way to go.

Keep Doing It

You cannot expect that altering your behavior on a few occasions will eliminate distrust that has built up over years. If you are prone to anger, derogation, or lying, your partner will still anticipate it even after you have begun to change. To eliminate distrust you must become consistent over a significant amount of time. Your partner's emotional brain will keep looking for evidence of the threat. Only after many months of reliability will your partner's emotional brain begin to relax and believe that the change is real. Then your partner's perception of you will change. You will no longer be the enemy. You will be perceived as more responsive. You will be perceived as more caring. The barriers to closeness will be gone.

Be Prepared for Backsliding

Unfortunately, there will be backsliding. We humans are not perfect. We are creatures of habit. There will be stressful moments when we regress back to the old negative behavior. When we backslide all the old tension in the relationship will return, and we must start the process all over again. This will be discouraging, but don't let your discouragement defeat you. Change is not easy. Progress is a jagged path. It involves two steps forward and one step back. You must be committed to the long haul.

Overcoming Emotional Obstacles to Change

Often, in order to change their behavior, spouses must overcome internal emotional obstacles. Let's consider some of these obstacles.

"It's Not Fair! Why Should I Have to Change?"

Your *Protector* would have you believe that you are being victimized by your partner's bad behavior. So why should you be the one to change? Your bad partner should change, not you. This pattern of thinking keeps many people stuck and miserable. If you believe that changing your own behavior will kill the TRAP pattern, then be pragmatic and do what it takes. *Protector* loves it when spouses get stuck on the mindset: "It isn't fair, why should I have to change?" Don't let *Protector* win.

"Doing What My Partner Wants Means that I am Being Controlled"

For many, being controlled feels like death itself. *Protector* wants you to feel threatened and resist being controlled. Actually, avoiding what threatens your partner puts you in control. You are in control of the TRAP sequence. If you become more responsive to your partner, you become the master of your marital bubble.

"I Already Have Too Much to Do!"

Protector loves laziness and inertia. It keeps people from changing. Sometimes the inner obstacle to change is that it requires effort. It means exerting oneself. Many spouses feel they already have too much to do. They feel overextended. They feel exhausted. Adding to their burden by engaging in greater relationship awareness and self-monitoring seems like too much. It isn't! It just feels that way. What spouses who feel this way need to understand is that it is far more exhausting to deal with TRAP sequences than it is to summon the energy to avoid them.

"I Can't Control Myself"

Many spouses know they lack self-control. They would like to be less impulsive and less explosive. They just don't believe it is possible. However, spouses can learn to be more in control of themselves through awareness and preparation. If they think about their behavior, monitor themselves, and anticipate the choice points, they will be able to maintain self-control.

Summary

To change your threatening behaviors you must do the following:

- Become more aware of the relationship.
- Monitor yourself for threatening behavior.
- Recognize the choice point.
- Ask, "What are the consequences of my behavior?"
- Make the right choice.

In the next chapter we will consider how to change Step #2 and Step #3 behaviors in the TRAP sequence. In subsequent chapters we will describe how spouses use all of these approaches in order to avoid their TRAP sequences.

Exiting Arguments by Using
Protector to Your Advantage

This book is about how to avoid arguments. However, all arguments cannot be avoided. When you find yourself in the middle of one, your goal should be to limit the damage by getting out of it as quickly as possible.

The key to exiting an argument is to avoid being provoked. If you can remain non-defensive you can avoid Step 2 behaviors. You accomplish this by becoming a sophisticated user of *Protector*. In other words, you can get *Protector* to work for your relationship, rather than against it.

You can use *Protector* to have a reassuring inner dialogue that neutralizes the moment of emotional pain brought on at Step 1. But let us be clear! The approaches described below are difficult! It is far better to spare your partner and yourself from having to employ them by avoiding the argument altogether.

Using *Protector* to Neutralize a Moment of Emotional Pain

At a moment of emotional pain, you experience a sudden drop in self-esteem. You may feel shame, guilt, or fear. Having an inner conversation that reminds you of your self-worth can neutralize the pain. This dialogue must be internal. If you make the dialogue external, you will start a TRAP sequence. If the dialogue remains internal, it will allow you to remain calm and will give you time to find a way out of the argument.

Below are three techniques that use *Protector* in this sophisticated way. They are **depersonalization, self-validation** and **perspective-taking.** We will discuss the depersonalizing technique first. But before we do so we must first discuss to tendency all of us have to personalize, thus making depersonalization necessary.

Personalizing

Some refer to personalizing as self-referencing. As discussed earlier, it is our automatic tendency to relate the upsetting events we experience to ourselves. Because our brains cause us to self-reference, we automatically ask, "What does this situation mean for me?"

Consider the following example: You are on your morning walk and you see a tiger crossing your path. When you see the tiger, you don't think to yourself, "There is a tiger on the path; the circus must be in town." Instead you think, "There is a tiger. I am in danger and must protect myself."

A similar sort of personalizing occurs in marriage. If your spouse has a scowl on her face, you may say to yourself, "She looks irritated; she must be working too hard." But just as likely you may personalize and think to yourself *"Her scowl must mean that she is mad at me— what have I done wrong?"* We humans are prone to personalizing and making these unwarranted assumptions.

Depersonalizing

Depersonalizing: It May Not Be About You

When we depersonalize we break the connection between the negative behavior of others and our thoughts about ourselves. You are capable of depersonalizing when you notice your spouse's scowl and refrain from making an assumption about what it means. Instead, you may inquire, "Are you upset about something?" You may learn it is not about you.

Consider the following example:

Giles and Melinda were exhausted after several stressful days selling one house, buying another, packing, and moving. Now, they stood alone in their new house and faced the task of unpacking. Giles hated the chaos of cardboard boxes scattered throughout the house. He wanted them gone as soon as possible. Melinda hated the dingy color of the walls. She wanted to repaint them immediately. When she decided to attack the walls instead of the boxes, Giles began to get angry and thought to himself, "She is against me." Then he caught himself and was able to depersonalize. He recognized that she was simply disturbed by different aspects of the situation than he was. She could tolerate the boxes, but not the walls. He was the opposite. She may have chosen to deal with the walls rather than the boxes, but acting on her own needs did not mean she was against him. Recognizing this allowed Giles to avoid a TRAP sequence.

Depersonalizing Self-Esteem Threats

Personalizing is even more destructive because not only do we ask, "Is this situation about me?", but we also ask, "What does this situation say about my worthiness or competence? Is my self-respect involved?" When you depersonalize a self-esteem threat you employ *Protector* in a sophisticated way to recognize that the situation has no bearing on your self-respect—your worth as a human being.

Consider this example: Your spouse forgets your birthday. Although this situation happens to you, it says nothing about your self-worth. Your partner hasn't forgotten your birthday because you are unworthy of being remembered. Your partner may have forgotten because she gets stressed, self-preoccupied, and forgets about other people.

It is bad enough that your partner has been oblivious to your birthday. But that is about your partner, not you. Don't make it worse by suddenly feeling that you are not worthy of being acknowledged. If you are a sophisticated user of *Protector* you can say to yourself: "This doesn't reflect on me. It happened to me, but is not about me." This must be an inner, not an external dialogue.

Self-Validation

Self-validation adds to depersonalization. When you engage in self-validation you engage in an inner dialogue that reminds you of your self-worth. Consider the following inner dialogue a spouse might engage in when the partner has been neglectful or critical:

"My partner has done something hurtful and I am feeling upset. Perhaps I did something that offended my partner. I have my faults. I am not perfect. But basically I am a good, decent person. Many people value me. Even if my spouse is angry at me right now, I remain okay. He may judge me, but I know I am a decent, worthwhile person."

At the moment of emotional pain, *Protector* will urge you to lash out at your partner with some sort of accusation that makes you feel better. However, a sophisticated use of *Protector* involves keeping the dialogue internal and using it to remain calm. In the following table are some examples of self-validating inner dialogues.

Self-Validating Inner Dialogues

The Threatening Behavior	The Moment Of Emotional Pain	The Self-Validating Inner Dialogue
Lack of support: You ask for help and your partner forgets to help.	My partner doesn't care about me.	I don't know why my partner forgot, but I know I am worth being helped (Self-validation). This says something about him, not me (Depersonalization). I will mention it, but I won't make an accusation because I don't want to start a TRAP sequence.
Criticism: Your partner gets frustrated and calls you stupid.	My partner has no respect for me.	My partner said this about me, but it is not about my intelligence, it is about his frustration (Depersonalization). I do many things well. I know I am not stupid (Self-Validation). I won't engage in name calling because that will trigger a TRAP sequence.
Coercion: Your partner repeatedly insists that you do something her way.	My partner thinks I can't think for myself and that I don't know what I am doing.	I know I can make my own decisions. I can also allow other people to be in control sometimes. That isn't a sign of weakness; it is a sign of smartness.
Withdrawal: You fear that if you speak up about what you want, your partner will be angry.	If my partner gets angry with me, that makes me a bad person. I will be alone.	It is inevitable that occasionally people will get angry if I speak up. Expressing myself doesn't make me bad. If my partner gets angry with me, she will get over it. I can survive on my own until she gets over it (Self-Validation).
Jealousy: My partner is paying too much attention to someone else.	My partner is more interested in that person than in me. My marriage is threatened.	If my partner talks to someone else, this has nothing to do with his feelings for me (Depersonalization). He loves me and values our relationship (Self-Validation). Paying attention to someone else doesn't change that.

Exercise 10: Inoculate Yourself against Your Worst Argument

Reconsider Exercise 9 (p. 60). Think about what your spouse does during Steps 1, 2 or 3 that you find most hurtful. Think about the feelings it stirs up. Why does it feel hurtful? Does it cause you to feel disrespected or unimportant? Or is it something else related to your personal history of emotional pain? Whatever it is, list it below under the painful feeling.

The painful feeling elicited by my partner's behavior is

_____

_____

Now consider the things you most value about yourself that are relevant. If you feel disrespected, think of the ways in which people have respected you. If you feel unimportant, think of the ways in you are important to others. List these thoughts under thoughts that contradict the painful feeling.

Thoughts that contradict the painful feeling:

_____

_____

_____

_____

_____

Use the thoughts that contradict the painful feeling to create a depersonalizing, self-validating inner dialogue.

_____

_____

_____

_____

As you imagine your partner engaging in the upsetting behavior from Exercise 9 (p. 60), use the depersonalization and self-validation inner dialogue techniques. Remind yourself that you are okay regardless of what your spouse says. Engage in this process repeatedly until you feel prepared for the situation.

Let's reconsider Alexander and Sophia (pp. 61-63).

Alexander was tired of their repetitive driving argument. He worked on developing a self-validating inner dialogue that he could use at moments when his wife began directing his driving.

The painful feeling: *She thinks I am irresponsible. This makes me feel like a stupid child. Am I?*

Alexander needed to remind himself of the ways in which he was responsible. In this situation, the relevant characteristics that he valued about himself were as follows:

Thoughts that contradict the painful feeling:

- I am an experienced driver.
- I see everything on the highway.
- I have never been in a serious accident.
- People respect my judgment.
- I do not put people in danger.

He turned these into the following self-affirming inner dialogue: "I am a good driver. I have never been in a serious accident. I am alert. I am aware of where the other cars are. I drive defensively. Everything is fine."

In order to prepare, Alexander imagined being in the car with his wife. He imagined his wife criticizing his driving. He used his inner dialogue. He did so repeatedly. When the time came, he had his self-affirming inner dialogue ready. When criticized, he used his inner dialogue to remain calm. The argument did not escalate.

Perspective-Taking

If you remain calm, you may be able to engage in perspective-taking, or what some refer to as empathy. Perspective-taking takes you out of your own world and into the inner world of your partner. It involves trying to understand this alien creature you are married to. If you remain calm you can consider your partner's motives, what your partner is feeling, and the possibility of your partner's emotional pain.

A perspective-taking inner dialogue would be as follows. "My partner just did something hurtful to me. What would motivate him or her to act like that? Is something stressing her out? What has happened to him today? Did she have a bad day? Is he hungry? Tired? Frustrated? What is he thinking? Has some core value has been violated? What is her view of this situation? What is she feeling? Has he just experienced a moment of emotional pain?

Consider how a perspective-taking inner dialogue might occur with regard to the threatening behaviors discussed above:

Lack of Support

My partner has hurt my feelings by failing to be supportive. I needed something from him and he let me down. He obviously wasn't thinking of me when I wanted him to be. What was my partner thinking about? What was so important that she didn't think to help? What is going on inside my partner's head? What motivates my partner?

Criticism

My partner has just said something that caused me to feel demeaned. This criticism puts my partner in the one-up position. Why does my partner want to be in this position? Is my partner feeling inferior or unworthy in some way? Does my partner need a self-esteem boost? Is my partner using me to feel better about herself? What is she feeling unworthy about? Is my partner experiencing a moment of emotional pain?

Control

My partner is being bossy. My partner is acting like it is "my way or the highway." Why is it so difficult for my partner to give up control? Does he feel anxious when not in control? What is she afraid of when not in control? What is it like for my partner to feel this way? Not very good, I would guess.

Withdrawal

My partner has withdrawn and won't talk to me. What is he feeling? Is my partner afraid of my disapproval or anger? What is so scary to my partner that she must retreat like this? What is it like to be locked up inside yourself like that? Not very good, I would guess.

Angry Outbursts

My partner is getting angry. Her voice is getting loud. Her face is turning red. You can see veins sticking out in her forehead. What is my partner experiencing? Does she feel that I am intentionally disregarding her? Does my partner feel unloved? What is making my partner feel this way? Is this a moment of emotional pain for my partner? Whatever it is, it is clearly upsetting her.

Lying

My partner is not telling me the truth. Is he ashamed of what he has done? Is he afraid of my reaction? Does he think I would get angry if I knew the truth? What is it like for my partner to lie? Does my partner feel guilty? Does my partner feel alone? He is probably not feeling very good right now.

Jealousy

My partner is jealous because I spent too much time with X. Does she think that my talking to X means that I prefer X? Does my partner think I would leave her for X? What does that feel like, I wonder? It probably feels bad.

Understanding Your Partner's Inner Experience

Focusing on your partner's inner experience may help you understand more clearly what is actually going on within your partner. This information can help you avoid a misunderstanding. In addition, by shifting your focus away from yourself, you give yourself time to regain your calm and defuse the situation.

Consider the following example:

Ordinarily, Ralph was a placid guy. However, during tax season his work load tripled. As April 15 approached he would become irritable and lash out. His wife didn't like this. She had been through this yearly ritual before and didn't look forward to it. Although Ralph never said he was stressed out during the tax season, she could tell from his body language and the intonation of his voice. She knew him well.

On this evening she could see that he was becoming agitated. When he lost it and yelled at her because of a mess in the kitchen, she wasn't surprised. This could easily have become Step 1 in a TRAP sequence. However, it did not because she engaged in the following perspective-taking: "He is obviously upset. What is he feeling? I don't think it is about the mess in kitchen. I think he is upset about all the tax returns he has not yet finished."

His wife's perspective-taking helped her remain calm. She didn't feel the need to defend herself and the situation did not escalate. Ten minutes later Ralph felt remorse over losing his temper and apologized. Consider the following example:

Tim had a high sex drive. Sex was usually on his mind. However, there were often times when he knew sex wasn't going to happen. His wife had been sexually molested as a child. Sometimes, her traumatic sexual memories remained dormant and she could enjoy sex with Tim. However, if she felt pressured to have sex, the early memories would become active and the thought of sex would become repulsive to her.

Tim had listened to his wife as she tried to explain her complicated feelings about sex. Although he knew he could never fully understand what she had gone through, he did recognize that for his wife sometimes sex could be frightening. When she rejected his sexual advances, he could easily have become angry and over-reacted. Instead, he engaged in the following perspective-taking to remain calm: "She is uptight right now. This is not about me. Her early memories are active and she feels distrustful. I need to back off."

As a result of his perspective-taking, Tim didn't feel rejected by his wife and didn't over-react. They successfully avoided making sex into a battleground.

Exercise 11: How Well Do You Know Your Partner?

What most upsets your partner?

_____

_____

What most worries your partner?

_____

_____

What most excites your partner?

_____

_____

What most frustrates your partner?

_____

_____

What most relaxes your partner?

_____

_____

What does your partner most yearn for?

_____

_____

What were your partner's moments of emotional pain as a child?

_____

_____

Reiteration

The general outline for a self-affirming internal dialogue is as follows: My partner has done something to hurt my feelings. I don't like it, but my partner's behavior says nothing about me or my self-worth. I am fine. I wonder what my partner might be feeling that caused her to behave this way. Whatever it is, I suppose my partner is not feeling very good right now.

What Happens When You Can Remain Calm

When you remain calm the following become possibilities:

- You might be able to avoid defensive accusations and derogatory language. This could be sufficient to defuse the argument.

- You might be able to show concern for your partner. You might be able to show that you are aware of what is upsetting your partner. If you communicate that you care about what is upsetting your partner, your partner may calm down.

- You might feel remorse. If you genuinely regret having engaged in a negative behavior, you might be able to overcome your *Protector* and apologize.

- You might comment on the presence of the TRAP sequence. You might recognize that the two of you are going down the same old miserable road. You might say, "Here we go again; do we really want to do this?"

- You might be able to let go of the issue and do nothing. **When angry, doing nothing is better than doing something.** Doing nothing might mean letting go and saying nothing. It might mean changing the subject. It could mean finding an excuse to exit the situation.

More Reiteration

The following diagram summarizes what you need to be thinking about to avoid TRAP sequences.

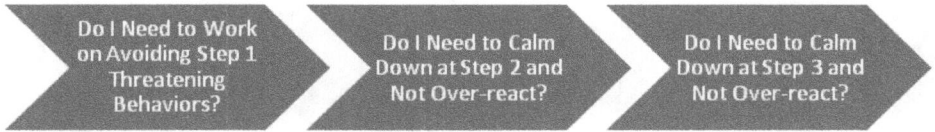

Do I Need to Work on Avoiding Step 1 Threatening Behaviors?	Do I Need to Calm Down at Step 2 and Not Over-react?	Do I Need to Calm Down at Step 3 and Not Over-react?

Fig. 6-2: What Do You Need To Work On?

In the next chapter we will examine a typical escalating argument. Then we will consider how the spouses might have defused it at Steps 2, 3 and beyond by using depersonalization, self-validation and perspective-taking.

The Argument

Let us consider a typical argument and how Hilda and Franz could have used depersonalization, self-validation and perspective-taking to exit it. The argument began during a visit from Hilda's parents. Her parents' visits always created additional tension. If the couple had more relationship awareness, they could have said to themselves "These visits are tense, we must be extra-careful with one another." Had they done so, perhaps they could have avoided their arguments. Unfortunately, they did not. The visits inevitably caused problems.

In this instance, Hilda had asked Franz to stay home with her parents and the kids while she went to an appointment. Although they had not discussed it, she assumed that her parents, Franz, and the kids would spend the afternoon together. While she was gone, Franz decided to leave Hilda's parents at home and take the kids to McDonalds for lunch. If he had engaged in perspective taking and considered the consequences, he might have anticipated that Hilda would not be happy with this. Unfortunately he didn't. Consider what happened as they discussed this issue with their therapist.

Therapist: How did it start?

Franz Excludes Her Parents

Franz: I mentioned to her that I had left her parents at home and had taken the kids to lunch.

Hilda felt that by leaving her parents behind Franz had shown disrespect for her and her family. Feeling demeaned and hurt by this exclusion, her Protector became involved and she made an accusation.

Hilda Called Franz "Selfish"

Therapist: What happened then?

Franz: She got mad. She called me selfish for doing that.

By calling Franz "selfish" Hilda tried to shift the painful sense of feeling disrespected from herself to Franz. Hilda's Protector is trying to establish the following: it is not that my family is unworthy of respect; it is that Franz is selfish and "bad." Temporarily, this helped Hilda feel better—but only until Franz reacted.

Franz Defended Himself and Minimized Her Feelings

Therapist: What did you say?

Franz: I said that it was no big deal. They were fine.

Franz's defensive counter-response was to minimize the importance of his behavior. If her parents were not impacted by his behavior, then he couldn't have done anything "bad." However, he didn't acknowledge Hilda's feelings. Hilda felt that she had been disregarded again. Thus, her Protector had Hilda go on the attack, leading to the next TRAP sequence.

Therapist: What happened then?

Hilda Criticized

Franz: She got angrier. She said that it was no way to treat any guest, let alone her parents.

Franz is accused and again must defend himself.

Therapist: What did you say?

Franz Counter-criticized

Franz: I said she had done worse things to my parents.

Under greater attack, Franz, aided by Protector, tries a new maneuver by counter-criticizing.

Hilda Defended

Franz: She demanded that I give her an example.

Therapist: What do you say?

Franz Counter-Accused

Franz: I brought up the time when my parents came over during dinner time and she had them sit in another room until we were finished eating. She could have invited them to the table.

Therapist: What did Hilda say?

Hilda Defended

Franz: She said she never did that.

This defensive denial makes Franz angry.

Franz and Hilda are now out of control. The TRAP sequence is controlling the interaction.

Therapist: What did you say?

Franz Escalated the Accusation

Franz: I said she did do it.

Therapist: What did Hilda say?

Hilda Derogated Franz

Franz: She called me a liar. That really pissed me off. I walked away from her.

Therapist: What happened then?

Franz: She said she is sick of my running away from situations.

Franz Withdrew and Punished Hilda

Franz: I was mad. I went to the basement and stayed there.

Following this interaction Hilda and Franz both felt hopeless. It seemed that all they did was argue. Each felt victimized by the other. Each selectively remembered how they had been attacked. Both forgot how each had also been on the attack. As a result, they were guarded around one another for days.

Breaking The TRAP Pattern:
What Else Could They Have Said?

The main point of this book is that this argument could have been avoided if Franz had understood what might lead to a TRAP sequence and avoided it. By recognizing the choice point, summoning the energy, and taking her parents with him, he would have avoided Hilda's hurt feelings. It is far easier to avoid a TRAP sequence than to try to escape from one.

However, once the TRAP sequence started, Franz and Hilda still could have escaped from it by avoiding threatening behaviors that escalated the conflict.

Let us consider what they might have done:

Franz Excludes Her Parents: Avoiding Feeling Disrespected through Perspective-Taking

Hilda felt disrespected when Franz excluded her parents. Did Franz's behavior really mean that he had no respect for Hilda and her family? Probably not. Had Hilda engaged in perspective-taking she might have concluded one of the following:

- Maybe he was in a bad mood that day and was afraid he would be rude to them.
- Maybe he was actually trying to protect them from disrespect by leaving. Franz didn't say that, but then again, Franz didn't usually share his feelings.
- Maybe one of the kids was acting up and Franz wanted to get him away from her parents.
- Maybe her parents really didn't want to go along. Perhaps they also needed some time away from Franz and the kids.

- Maybe Franz really does have respect for Hilda and her family. Perhaps Hilda needed to remind herself of the acts of kindness Franz had performed for her parents.

Had Hilda done any of the above, she may have reacted differently.

Hilda Called Franz Selfish: Escaping the TRAP Sequence by Avoiding Derogation

Hilda got upset and called Franz "selfish," thus eliciting his defensiveness. If Hilda had been more aware of the consequences of her behavior, she could have thought about how to make her point without being derogatory. Franz may have been thoughtless, but if Hilda understands the TRAP sequence, she will realize that it is futile to try to get him to consider his thoughtlessness by insulting him. Hilda could have said, "That is no way to treat a guest," and left out the inflammatory accusation that he had been "selfish."

Franz Minimized Hilda's Feelings: Escaping the TRAP sequence by Showing Concern and Apologizing

Hilda got more upset when Franz minimized her feelings. He implied that it was no big deal, thus escalating the argument. What could Franz have done differently? Instead of minimizing her concern, he could have expressed awareness of his wife's feelings. He could have acknowledged that his wife was upset and apologized.

As we know, *Protector* hates apologizing since it implies wrongdoing. However, if Franz could realize that *Protector* is not helpful, perhaps he could rise above *Protector* and acknowledge that he had made a mistake.

He could have said, "I am sorry, I didn't realize this would upset you." *Any acknowledgement of Hilda's unhappiness would probably have ended the* TRAP sequence. Showing concern for the partner's feelings works like magic. However, when threat is present, this simple act is quite difficult. *Protector* is on guard and will try to prevent it.

Franz Counter-Criticized: Escaping the TRAP sequence by Depersonalizing and Doing Nothing

Hilda called Franz "selfish." How will he react to this accusation? If the threat level is high, he will probably defend himself with a counter-accusation. However, if he has his wits about him, if he understands the futility of the TRAP sequence, then he can choose to behave differently.

He could work at self-validation and perspective-taking. He could remind himself of all the unselfish things he had done for his wife. He could recognize that she says things she doesn't mean when she is angry. Or, he could recognize that because he is upset, it is best to say nothing.

Franz could do nothing by side-tracking the conversation. He could offer a lame excuse that gets him out of the situation. He could say to Hilda, "I need to make a phone call; I need to go to the bathroom; or I need to check the hot water heater. Let's get back to this conversation later." These are odd responses to be sure, but they prevent the unhappy consequence of a TRAP sequence.

Escaping the TRAP Sequence by Commenting on its Presence

If Franz has his wits about him, he could also comment directly on what is going on. He could say, "Here we go again. We are about to get into mutual name calling. Let's not go there. We have been down that road before and it gets ugly." He could say, "Can we discuss this later when we are calm?"

Unfortunately, Franz does none of these things. Instead, with his *Protector* in control, Franz attempts to transfer his bad feelings from himself to his wife. His message to Hilda is—"You have done bad things too." How will Hilda react to this counter-accusation? Chances are she will defend herself. But she does not have to.

Hilda Defended Herself: Escaping the TRAP Sequence through Depersonalizing and Self-Validation

If Hilda could remain calm long enough to engage in self-validation and perspective-taking, she might realize that Franz has accused her because he feels guilty and defensive. Recognizing this can help her keep her *Protector* in check.

Hilda could also say to herself: "His accusation is directed at me, but it is not really about me. Franz is feeling guilty. He just said that to defend himself. I know that I am not a selfish person. I know I am thoughtful of others. I know my value as a human being. There is no reason to get upset by his accusation. It is groundless." This is clearly difficult to accomplish when you are fending off threat. But it can be done.

Recognizing the futility of the TRAP sequence, Hilda could also choose to do nothing. She could let go of it. She could change the subject and say, "What else went on today?" She could be conciliatory and say, "You are not selfish; I was just frustrated that you left them behind." She can comment on the TRAP pattern and say, "Here we go again. Do we want to get into argument again?"

If spouses are capable of calming themselves down, there is no end to the creative ways they can come up with to escape from TRAP patterns.

| 8 | Sam and Diane Overcome A Lack of Support/Anger/Defensiveness Trap |

Sam and Diane were an attractive couple. They met when they were in the military. After getting out, they settled in the South where Sam continued his career in information systems. When the children came along Diane stayed at home.

They were outgoing, friendly, and easy to talk to. If you met them at a party, you would like them. You would assume that they were happily married. They were not! If you saw how they behaved in the marital bubble, you would not like them. The TRAP sequences made them mean and unpleasant.

Diane's complaints were typical of what brings many wives into marital therapy: Sam didn't help; he didn't share his feelings, they never went anywhere; all he cared about was his work. Diane felt disregarded. To her, Sam's disengaged behavior could only mean that he didn't care about her. She had voiced her concerns repeatedly, but Sam remained defensive and unresponsive. As her anger mounted, she became more attacking and Sam became more withdrawn.

Sam's complaints were also fairly typical. He felt his wife was always angry. He felt she was overly critical. He felt she was not interested in sex. Sam was angry that she didn't appreciate how hard he worked for his family.

Sam's and Diane's *Protectors* each reacted violently to the other's complaints. The *Protector* within each helped them come to the same conclusion: "It is not me. There is nothing wrong with me. My partner is the mean and selfish one."

They had become embroiled in a classic TRAP pattern. Sam was not aware of his lack of support at Step 1. However, he was aware of his wife's behavior at Step 2: her chronic anger and accusations. He felt under constant attack. At Step 3 he minimized his wife's concerns and withdrew. This generated greater anger within Diane and more withdrawal by Sam. It was a vicious cycle that neither could escape from.

Their Background and Gender Differences

Neither Diane nor Sam had difficult backgrounds. Growing up, they felt cared for. There had been few moments of emotional pain. But they were feeling emotional pain now. It was their socialization differences and their differing expectations about marriage that contributed to their arguments.

Diane's Socialization

Women are better prepared for marriage by early socialization. They have been practicing caring and support for most of their lives. Diane was no exception. When Diane was a child her mother had certain expectations about how she would behave. Her mother made sure that those expectations were met. Diane was to be polite. Diane was to think of others. Diane was to be helpful.

If Diane deviated from these expectations, her mother's disapproval was a powerful and unsettling force. But there was little need for disapproval since Diane learned her role well. She was usually a sweet and respectful child. She was aware of the needs of others and was eager to please them. Her relatives and teachers sang her praises.

Diane's interactions with her young female friends reinforced her orientation toward others. As they played together, they alternated in roles of eager speaker and interested listener. Sometimes they played games. Sometimes they just talked. Demonstrating support and caring was a central aspect of these interactions and became a core aspect of Diane's identity. It was a quality she came to value in herself and in others. When Diane married she expected that her husband would share this orientation. Sometimes he did, sometimes he didn't.

Sam's Socialization

Being supportive and caring was part of Sam's socialization as well. But it was a less central part. Sam's mother raised her daughters the way Diane's mother did. But Sam's mother had a different set of expectations for Sam. She wanted him to be independent and self-reliant. Whereas Diane was encouraged to depend on her mother, Sam was raised to move away from that kind of dependency and to develop autonomy. For example, when Sam's sisters would complain about mistreatment by peers, his mother was sympathetic. When Sam complained about this, she told him to deal with it.

Sam's relationship with his male friends was also different. The focus of their interaction was more external. They came together to play a competitive game or to collaborate on a project. Caring and sharing was not a central focus. Engaging in tasks and games was a way of preparing Sam to function independently in a competitive world. The pressure that Sam received from his parents was to learn to control his emotions so that he could successfully compete.

Sam learned his role well. He developed the self-control necessary to sit alone at his desk until his schoolwork was finished. His grades pleased his parents and earned their praise. When his football coach encouraged him to be aggressive and to push through physical pain, he did so. This too won him admiration and praise.

While Sam's ability to function autonomously and exert self-control helped him in the competitive world of work, it did not prepare him to function well in marriage. Sam was task oriented. Sam had less experience monitoring his behavior and considering the feelings of others. Marriage is about mutual concern. Excessive autonomy gets in the way.

Patriarchy

Diane and Sam both came from families that had been somewhat patriarchal. Family life had been organized around their fathers. The father's job and his needs came first. Sam's family was particularly hierarchical. His father was at the top of the hierarchy, followed by his mother, then Sam, and then younger siblings. Privileges and responsibilities were determined by rank. Opinions that went against the family belief system were not permissible in Sam's family. Overt anger was particularly taboo. Conflicts between family members were resolved by relative rank. If you were higher, you prevailed. This allowed conflicts to be resolved without confrontation. In Sam's family you knew when to push and when to back off.

Although somewhat patriarchal, Diane's family was more democratic. Family members felt freer to express themselves. Diane, as the first born, was particularly outspoken. Sam was not prepared to deal with this aspect of Diane's personality. She had not been so outspoken during the euphoria of the romantic phase.

Sam's and Diane's mothers did not work. Their job had been managing the home and the events of daily life such as carpooling, helping with homework, giving baths, cooking, shopping, and cleaning. If the role assigned to these women seemed unfair, they never said so overtly. It was a different time.

Sam worked full time. Diane worked part-time. Despite Diane's job, Sam was automatically prepared to assume that his marriage would be like his parents' marriage. Initially, Diane went along with this. However, in contemporary life, patriarchy has been trumped by the notion of equality. The inequity Diane experienced eventually began to bother her.

Moralistic Rage

In today's marriages many wives are chronically angry at their husbands over the issue of inequity, and their husbands are on the defensive. This anger can be understood as an expression of moralistic rage. Moralistic rage is the anger spouses feel when their partners violate their deeply held beliefs about how people should behave.

How do you become a good person from the female perspective? You do this by being responsive; by sharing, by caring, by helping; by cooperating; by being a team player. Women want their husbands to think the way they do and behave the way they do.

When wives see their husbands behave in ways they define as unsupportive or disengaged, they become furious. They become furious not simply because they feel disregarded and experience a moment of emotional pain. They also become furious because they think that their husbands are engaging in "bad" behavior—behavior that violates basic core beliefs about how to interact with others.

This is often not clear to their husbands. Husbands hear their wives' complaints. They know their wives are angry. However, they do not fully understand what the anger is about. As a result, they do not take the complaints they hear seriously.

In the case of Sam and Diane, Sam's failure to understand Diane's orientation toward marriage became the central problem. A significant focus in their marital therapy was on helping Sam understand his wife and on helping Sam to become more engaged and responsive, thus avoiding threatening behavior and subsequent TRAP sequences.

The First Session

The day of the session had been stressful for both. Diane was angry that Sam left the house without saying goodbye. She was angry that she had to be in two places at once: her middle daughter had a gymnastics class at the same time her youngest daughter had a dental appointment.

That morning there had been a school conference for her oldest daughter. The guidance counselor thought the oldest daughter was depressed. Diane wanted to discuss this with Sam, but she couldn't. He hadn't answered his cell phone. Diane was feeling alone. If Sam cared, she thought to herself, his cell phone would have been on. "All he cares about is work," she concluded. Her glare was powerful as she sat across from the therapist.

Sam came to the session from work. He was fifteen minutes late and he looked harassed. Nothing had gone right that day. Some of his staff was out sick. His boss had ignored his advice on a project. He was behind on an assignment. As he anticipated the marital session, he knew he would have to deal with his wife's anger. He felt the knot tighten in his stomach as he entered the therapist's waiting room. When under stress, Sam felt it first in his stomach. He considered canceling the session and staying at work; however, he knew he that would get him in more trouble.

When the therapist asked about problems in their marriage, Diane began to unload her concerns. As Diane spoke, Sam listened uncomfortably. Sometimes he looked at Diane. Sometimes he stared at the floor. Being in the presence of her anger was difficult for him. He looked like a cornered animal.

When the therapist asked Sam what he thought about what he was hearing, Sam was slow to respond. Finally, he said that he didn't think it was as bad as Diane portrayed. He felt she made such a big deal out of insignificant issues. He said that he felt under tremendous pressure at work and wanted her to be more understanding.

Sam and Diane were clearly in a miserable rut. Each felt hurt and misunderstood. They were feeling hopeless about their relationship. However, it was clear that both wanted to improve their relationship and were willing to work on it.

To accomplish this, Sam and Diane were going to have to understand their TRAP patterns and work on changing their own behavior. Sam needed to replace Step 1, lack of support, with involvement and responsiveness. Diane needed to replace Step 2, her angry criticism, with control over her angry outbursts.

The Importance of Supportive Behavior

At the end of session one, the therapist asked Diane and Sam to fill out the Support List. Lack of support brings on TRAP sequences. Providing support avoids them. The Support List is a set of questions designed to unearth the kind of support a spouse wants from the partner. *If your partner perceives you as supportive you cannot be perceived as threatening.* Thus, you deprive TRAP sequences of their energy.

Here is what we know about support:

Supportive behavior is powerful! Adults who feel supported are insulated from loneliness, stress, mental and physical disease. Feeling support enhances self-esteem. It is also associated with greater marital satisfaction.

Spousal Support Resonates! Simple acts of support in marriage resonate with past nurturing experiences in childhood and adolescence. They resonate with those moments in infancy when your physical needs were attended to: when you were fed and caressed by a loving parent and you experienced contentment. They resonate with childhood situations when you demanded "watch me" and your empathic parent understood your need for admiration and supplied it. They resonate with times when you were hurt or upset and your parent was soothing.

All of these moments contribute to a sense of security and well being—what psychologists call secure attachment. Secure attachment involves being connected to someone who is responsive and reliable. As adults we retain this need for a secure attachment. It is mainly the spouse who provides it. Supportive behavior from a spouse can be an antidote for many of the painful experiences that occurred in childhood.

In marriage, support can occur in situations both profound and mundane. It can occur in a crisis when a spouse is frightened and needs help. It can occur when there is a loss and when connection to a spouse helps overcome loneliness.

Marital support can also occur during the daily trivia of life: it can occur when your partner listens to you, it can occur when you take out the trash; it can occur when you change a diaper; it can occur when you give your spouse time to relax. These acts maintain a "positive hum" in the relationship. They keep the "well-being" areas of your brain activated. They inhibit the threat centers.

Although the initial romantic attraction may be to the partner's sex appeal, charisma, humor, courage, power, etc. there is an implicit expectation that the partner can be counted on to be supportive, thus repeating the early nurturing interactions of our infancy and childhood. Unfortunately, this implicit expectation is often not met.

The Support List

Below, Diane and Sam indicated what kind of support they want with regard to the following: (1) the household; (2) parenting; (3) communicating; (4) companionship activities; (5) in-laws; (6) sex life; (7) alone time. After responding to the seven items they ordered them from most to least important.

Let's consider Diane's Support List.

1. Parenting: I want help with the kids—help with their homework and putting them to bed.

2. Household: I want help with the cleaning and keeping things organized. You leave your stuff everywhere.

3. Communication: I wish you would tell me more about how you feel.

4. In-Laws: I wish you wouldn't leave when we visit your family. I am stuck with your mother.

5. Alone Time: I wish you would watch the kids on the weekend and let me work in the garden.

6. Sex Life: I wish you would hold me when we are in bed without it being about sex.

7. Companionship Activities: I would like us to go for walks the way we used to.

Let's consider Sam's Support list.

1. Communication: I wish you didn't get so angry when we discuss things.

2. Sex Life: I wish you would show more interest in our sex life.

3. Companionship: I wish we could find time for a weekend away.

4. Alone Time: I would like time on the computer without being criticized.

5. Parenting: I want you to stop being so harsh with our daughter.

6. Household: I want you to stop criticizing the way I clean.

7. In-Laws: I don't have a problem with your parents.

The Support List Reveals Contributions to the TRAP Pattern

Was Sam contributing to his own marital unhappiness? Clearly, he was. His lack of involvement and his tendency to withdraw were eliciting the anger he so disliked. The question was could he rise above his *Protector* and see the connection between his behavior and his marital unhappiness?

Was Diane responsible for her own marital unhappiness? Clearly she was. Her anger was causing the disengagement she so disliked. To her, Sam was selfish and she had the right to be angry. Would Diane be able to rise above her *Protector* and see the connection between her behavior and her marital unhappiness?

They Discuss the Support Lists in a Session

Sam and Diane review their Support Lists.

Diane's List. What Diane wanted from Sam was more involvement in family life and less withdrawal. This is reflected in many of her items, including her highest ranked item—wanting help with the kids.

Sam was baffled by Diane's list. "What does wanting help with the kids have to do with our relationship?" he thought. He was hoping for something related to sex or companionship. The therapist tried to help him understand Diane's sense of inequity and frustration. As Sam listened, he felt he was being blamed for their problems. His *Protector* was getting agitated. He wanted to defend himself. Still, some of what Diane was saying was getting through.

Sam's List. First on Sam's list was that Diane be less critical and angry with him. Diane knew he felt this way, but she thought her anger was justified. "If Sam is selfish he deserves my anger. Why can't I express it?" she said. "You can if you want to," the therapist said, "but consider the consequences. When you get angry and criticize, he disengages. You create the very withdrawal you dislike. How does that help you?"

Diane's *Protector* was now getting agitated. According to her *Protector,* Sam was hypersensitive to criticism and should change. She wanted him to develop a thicker skin. The therapist said that it would be nice if Sam was less sensitive. But in reality that was unlikely. Sam is who he is. "It is better to work on getting the threat (angry criticism) out of the relationship," the therapist said.

Exercise 12: What Kind of Support
Do You Want from Your Partner?

Parenting

_____

_____

Household Chores

_____

_____

Communication

_____

_____

In-Laws

_____

_____

Alone Time

_____

_____

Sex Life

_____

_____

Companionship Activities

_____

_____

Finances

_____

_____

Other

_____

_____

They Commit to Their Tasks

Sam was willing to commit to helping more with homework and bedtime routines. He complained that in the past when he had helped with the kids, Diane would criticize how he did it. For example, Diane read books to them at bedtime. He did this as well. But he also told them stories. Diane didn't like this. She thought his stories got them riled up. He grew tired of her criticism and therefore stopped helping. Diane agreed to say nothing about how he dealt with them as long as he helped. In general, she committed to trying to be less critical.

Sam was a highly conscientious individual. When given an assignment he followed through. But Sam was also highly resistant to being controlled. The therapist wondered if Sam would feel coerced by the assignment and find ways to resist.

Following Up On the Support Lists

Sam Follows Up

During the next several sessions the therapist inquired about how things had gone. He was prepared for anything. Fortunately, in this case there was progress. Diane reported that Sam had helped with homework and bedtime. She had refrained from critiquing how he went about it.

"What was that like for you, when he helped?" the therapist asked. Diane said it felt better. She seemed pleased. "Did Diane seem any different?" the therapist asked Sam. Sam answered, "Perhaps a little calmer."

The therapist wanted to assess how controlled Sam felt by the assignment. "What is it like for you to do these things?" the therapist asked Sam. Sam didn't care for "what is it like for you" questions.

They felt intrusive to Sam. "It is not that different," Sam replied. "I usually do these things." The therapist got little information from Sam's response. Sam's *Protector* had controlled the response, which was defensive.

Despite his reticence, Sam seemed willing to go along with the therapist's plan. He seemed to be treating the therapist like a high school coach who had told him to do fifty pushups. That was fine for now. Eventually, Sam would have to see that his supportive behavior paid off. Otherwise he would stop helping.

Diane Follows Up

"How is it going with anger?" the therapist asked Diane. Diane said she was trying. She described an incident when Sam was late and didn't call to tell her. She felt this was inconsiderate. But she anticipated the consequences of saying so, recognized the choice point, and resisted the urge. Sam seemed surprised. He was not aware that she had done this. How could he be? When someone inhibits a criticism, the partner can't see the internal effort that went into it. Bringing it to the surface allowed Sam to see that Diane was trying.

Sam acknowledged that there had been less angry sniping. "What was that like?" the therapist inquired. Sam was able to say, "It felt better." "Do you think it is connected to your helping?" the therapist inquired. "Perhaps," Sam replied. Both left the session calmer. Each could tell the other was trying.

They continued to work on their assignments. Sam helped and he tried to stay engaged. Diane monitored her behavior and tried to edit out angry criticism. The therapist's guess was that in the course of the next several weeks they avoided several TRAP sequences. This was encouraging. But married life is cyclic. Things are good for awhile and then something triggers an argument. The therapist knew there would be backsliding. In this case it occurred on a night when Sam and Diane were out together.

Progress and Backsliding

They Go to a Concert

In the interest of improving their relationship, Diane and Sam decided to go to a concert. Both were in a good mood as they bought their tickets and headed to their seats. The trouble began when they both decided to go to the bathroom before sitting down. Sam got out of the bathroom first. He waited briefly for Diane. Then he decided he was hungry and wanted something to eat. He headed for the concession stand down the corridor.

Diane came out shortly thereafter and waited for her husband. When he failed to appear she began to worry. She stopped a man leaving the bathroom and asked if he had seen her husband in the bathroom. He said no. After several more minutes, fearing he had become ill, she opened the door to the men's room and shouted his name. No one answered. Now she began to panic. She was searching for a security guard when she spotted him with a hotdog.

Diane was furious. While she had been waiting for him, and worrying, he was off eating. "Typical selfishness," she said. "I would never do that." Sam was bewildered. "What have I done wrong? What is the big deal?" he wondered. This was typical of their gender-based conflicts. Sam, guided by his autonomy orientation, wandered off assuming his wife would find him. His relationally oriented wife assumed he would stay and wait. To her, that is what any good person would do.

Diane was angry and told him so! Sam, of course, felt attacked and became defensive. They argued and their evening together was ruined. In the days that followed the argument continued. Diane attacked—Sam defended—and they remained stuck in their positions.

When they appeared for the therapy session both looked grim. Sam's stomach hurt. Diane glowered. As they related what had occurred at the concert their *Protectors* were hard at work distorting the facts to their own advantage. It took the therapist a while to accurately piece together the sequence of events. When he did, he suggested that Sam's lack of awareness had been the problem. He said that Sam hadn't asked himself the crucial question about going off to look for food: "What will be the consequences of my behavior?" Had he done so, Step 1 could have been avoided.

Sam was upset! Despite this, he was able to rise above his *Protector*. He acknowledged that he could have handled the situation differently.

Sam is Aware of Diane's Day

Sam worked to become more aware of his wife's feelings and more aware of their interactions. Consider the following example. Sam was exhausted. He was late on a project and his boss was unhappy about it. He had a headache. As he approached home he anticipated his wife's glare and he began to feel the knot in his stomach.

He summoned the energy to stop thinking about his problems and began to consider his wife. He remembered that she was taking their daughter to the psychologist that day. He recognized that Diane would be angry if he didn't ask about it. To Diane, if he didn't ask it would mean he didn't care about his family. Sam knew that he cared about his family. He was beginning to recognize that he needed to show that he cared.

Sam entered the house and greeted his wife. She seemed all right. His stomach began to relax. A few minutes later he said, "How did the appointment with the doctor go?" Diane's had been waiting to see if he would ask. His question immediately calmed her. Diane began to describe the visit. His heightened awareness had allowed him to avoid a TRAP sequence. He was starting to make real progress.

Sam and Diane Go to the Mall

In the interest of building their relationship, Sam and Diane decided to go shopping together and then go out to lunch. Sam was wearing old sweat pants. Diane found this embarrassing. Diane could have criticized his clothes and badgered him until he changed. She could have lapsed into the following thought: "If he cared about my embarrassment he would change his clothes." But she did not go there. She recognized that acting on this thought could easily trigger a TRAP sequence. She decided to say nothing. She used depersonalizing and self-validation to help her. She said to herself: "I look presentable. I am okay. If he wants to look like a slob that is his problem, not mine." This inner dialogue helped her remain calm. They dodged another TRAP sequence.

Sam Snaps At Diane

Sam's work situation was worsening. He felt overwhelmed and stressed out. He had started to share more about his work concerns. That night Diane could see that he was upset and she understood why. They decided to watch a movie. When watching T.V., Diane had the habit of quickly switching to the Weather Channel and then back to the movie. That night, Sam snapped at her and said, "I hate it when you do that."

Diane's heightened awareness of her husband helped her depersonalize and remain calm. She said to herself, "I don't like being snapped at, but I am not going to take it personally. I know he is upset about work." This inner dialogue helped Diane maintain her equanimity and prevented her from over-reacting. Another TRAP sequence was avoided.

Things continued to improve for Diane and Sam. There was less threat in the marital bubble. Diane's glower was fading. Sam's stomach was in knots less often. However, it was still two steps forward and one step back.

Another Relapse: Who is in Control, Sam, Diane or the TRAP Sequence?

By now, Sam understood more clearly how important the issue of helping was to Diane. Guided by this, he offered to help Diane with dinner. Diane was pleased. She suggested that he cut up the vegetables.

As Sam began his task, Diane suggested a more efficient approach. She understood that Sam didn't like being controlled; however, she didn't see her behavior as controlling. She thought she was being helpful. Suddenly Sam felt he was being told what to do and how to do it. Momentarily, he had a feeling of incompetence: a moment of emotional pain. His *Protector* initiated flight! Sam told Diane to cut up her own vegetables and abruptly left the kitchen.

Diane felt blindsided and was furious. As she cut up the vegetables she regressed to her old inner dialogue, fueled by her *Protector*. The inner dialogue was, "He is a selfish jerk." Their argument about the incident lasted for several days. Neither could let go of it.

Their Murky Marital Reality

As they discussed the incident in therapy, their different realities became clear. Sam was convinced that Diane had been trying to control him. He desperately wanted her to admit it. Diane insisted she was only trying to be helpful. She desperately wanted him to see this.

Was Diane right? Had Sam misinterpreted her intent? Was Sam right? Was Diane unable to face up to her own need for control? Was this an aspect of her personality that her *Protector* would not let her see?

Sam, Diane and the therapist were in a murky place where nothing is clear. The therapist had visited this place many times with other couples. He knew that each had a partial claim on reality. Diane was partially right. Sam had misinterpreted Diane's intent. Her intent was to be helpful. However, Diane was like many other competent people. She liked things to be done right, i.e. her way. Her *Protector* wouldn't let her see that others often experienced her as domineering, regardless of her intent.

Both spouses wanted the therapist to validate their own view of reality. The therapist had still a third agenda. He wanted them to see the futility of their argument. Each wanted to win—neither would ever win. Their *Protectors* wouldn't let them. It was best that they agree to disagree. That was all they could hope for. But neither was in a mood to hear this. The TRAP pattern had control of them and wouldn't let go.

Both left the session angry. Neither could see that their argument was an exercise in futility. The therapist imagined that if he brought up this issue twenty years later they would still remember it and would still argue about it. Such is the nature of marriage. No argument ever completely dies in the marital bubble.

Despite this impasse they plowed ahead. Sam continued to help with the kids and tried to stay engaged. Diane monitored for angry criticism and tried to avoid it. The trend was upward.

Being Aware of Others

Sam and Diane were preparing breakfast. Sam was cutting up fruit for his cereal. In an earlier session, Diane had complained that when she cut up fruit, she cut up enough for everyone in the family. When Sam did it, he cut up enough fruit only for himself. "Why do you do this?" she asked. Sam replied that he had never thought about it. Sam remembered this conversation that Saturday morning. This time, he cut up enough fruit for all of them. Diane was pleased. So was Sam. The level of threat was going down.

Avoiding Hostile Sniping

Sam had asked Diane not to nag him after he had agreed to do a chore. He hated being nagged. Diane said that she nagged because he would forget if she didn't. In the past that had been true. Sam had actually brought the nagging upon himself, because he didn't follow through. However, over the past several months he had worked on becoming more reliable. Diane's trust was fragile, but growing.

Earlier that day they decided that Sam would move a bookshelf into their daughter's bedroom. Later in the day, Diane saw Sam playing games on the computer. She thought that this was a waste of time. In the past, Sam had tried to explain that it relaxed him, but Diane didn't understand.

Over the preceding months Diane could see that Sam had been trying to be more reliable. She knew she could elicit a TRAP sequence with one hostile remark about the computer games. At the choice point, she bit her tongue. When he was ready, Sam moved the bookshelf.

They Settle In

Maintaining their new behaviors was requiring less thought and energy. It was becoming easier to consider the consequences of their behavior and make the right choices. They were getting into a groove. They continued to have their ups and downs; however, the old days of constant arguing were gone. Sam and Diane were no longer enemies.

Is Your Marriage Like Sam And Diane's?

If your marriage is similar to Sam and Diane's, then consider doing what they did. Fill out the rating scales and identify your threatening behaviors. Identify the TRAP sequences. Is your own problematic behavior at Step 1 or Step 2 or Step 3? Is it your lack of support, your angry criticism, or your defensiveness that is contributing to the arguments?

Fill out the Support questionnaire and have your partner do likewise. Explain what you are looking for in the way of support. Determine what your partner is looking for regarding support. Try to increase your awareness of when support is called for.

Monitor yourself for the threatening behavior (lack of support, anger or defensiveness). Identify the choice points. Consider the consequences of your choices. Notice what happens when your behavioral choice takes you in one direction or the other. Try to use a self-affirming inner dialogue when your partner upsets you.

If things begin to improve, consider why. If you begin to make progress, be prepared for the ups and downs—and persevere.

9	Maria and Miguel Overcome A Silent Withdrawal TRAP

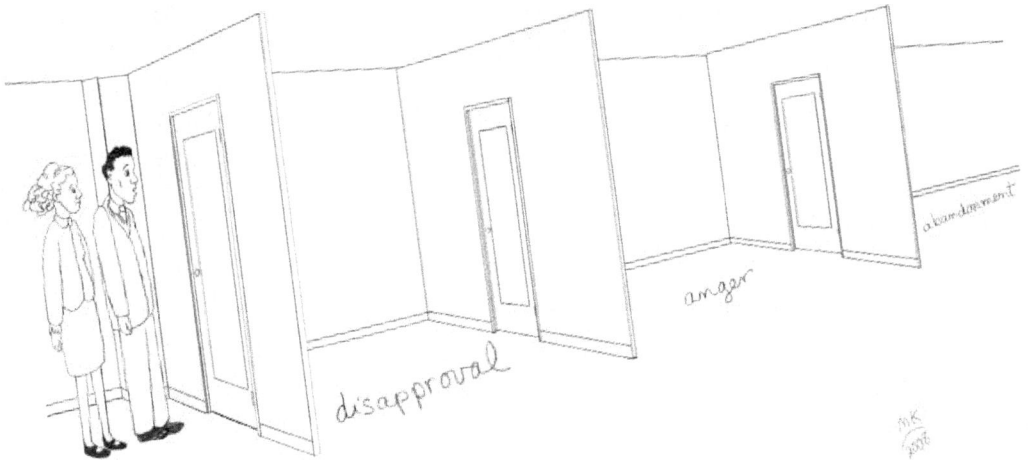

Communication Avoidance, Silence, and Threat

If spouses won't say what they want, resolving the clash of needs becomes impossible. Spouses still want what they want. They just won't say what it is. Because it is so hard for them to express themselves, they want their partners to know what they are thinking without having to say it. When the partner fails to read the spouse's mind, the spouse's resentment builds. In the absence of information the partner remains oblivious.

The oblivious partner may then act on his or her own needs and may come to be seen as selfish. Eventually the oblivious partner may begin to notice that the spouse is unhappy. The partner may begin to wonder what the spouse is unhappy about and will worry. Is she hiding anger, criticism, or contempt? The lack of information in the marital bubble becomes threatening. It breeds silent TRAP sequences.

As threat increases, the communication patterns may become even more vague and indirect. Misunderstandings and confusion follow. It may be apparent that a spouse is upset at the same time that she denies it. As the bubble fills with threat, silent withdraw/withdraw sequences predominate—each spouse withdraws in response to the other's withdrawal.

To avoid these silent TRAP sequences, spouses need to put more information into the marital bubble about what they want and how they feel. This chapter is about how to go about doing that. But first, let's explore why spouses won't say what it is that they want.

Why Spouses Won't Say What They Want: Fear of Disapproval and Anger

Everyone wants approval. As children we needed our parents' acceptance to feel safe. Their approval helped us feel good about ourselves. Experiencing their disapproval was uncomfortable. Our parents' approval and disapproval guided our behavior and helped us learn how to act appropriately.

As teenagers, pleasing our friends also became important. We recognized that there would be times when our parents would be unhappy with us. We could tolerate their unhappiness as long as we had the approval of our friends.

As we moved beyond the teenage years, we became more autonomous and less dependent on peer acceptance. We developed our own value systems and were guided more by our own beliefs. Eventually many of us became genuinely desirous of pleasing others because we wanted to, not because we couldn't tolerate their disappointment or anger.

Some of us never finished our progression through those stages. We became people pleasers—slaves to the need to maintain the approval of everyone. Such individuals will sacrifice their own needs in order to stay in the good graces of others. The mere hint of disapproval activates fear. As spouses we will freeze, stop thinking, stop feeling, and do whatever it takes to avoid the dreaded possibility of disapproval. The clash of needs is never resolved in our favor.

Why Spouses Won't Say What They Want: Feeling Unequal

Some of us avoid expressing our needs because we feel unequal. We see our partners as having a higher status. Sometimes we view our partners as more physically attractive, or more intelligent, or more educated, or better off financially, or more decisive. We are grateful the partner has chosen us for marriage. Because we view ourselves as "one down," we may feel less entitled to speak up and get what we want. Yet, we still want what we want. Our resentment builds.

Why Spouses Won't Say What They Want: Guilt

In some cases fear of not speaking up is based on guilt. Such spouses think that asserting their needs makes them selfish and bad. More often it is women who struggle with the guilt issue. Their early socialization experience has taught them to think of and meet the needs of others. Some learned this role too well. They come into marriage prepared to take care of their husbands and children, but ill equipped to take care of themselves.

Why Spouses Won't Say What They Want: Fear of Abandonment

Sometimes lack of assertiveness derives from deeper sources. Sometimes, it is based on a fear of being abandoned. This fear is present in all of us in infancy. As infants we were all helpless and dependent on our caregivers to feed and protect us. The greatest threat the infant faces is to be cut off physically from its caregiver. Without a connection to a nurturing adult we would have died.

In most animal species, including human beings, when the infant wanders off and loses sight of the mother, the panic areas of the infant's brain are activated. The terrified infant will wail in fear. This loud wailing helps the mother to locate the missing infant and allows for a reconnection. In this way, the feeling of panic has survival value.

As adults we can survive on our own. We don't need to depend on our spouses to survive. But that doesn't mean that the panic centers of our brains won't go off when we experience a sense of disconnection from our partners. In some vague inexpressible way, when the partner threatens to withdraw, it feels like our survival is at stake. Although we won't die without this sense of connection, for some of us, when the partner withdraws love the panic response remains.

Early Losses

The fear of abandonment is intensified for those who have had significant losses in childhood. For those spouses, the marital partner inadvertently takes on the role of the life-sustaining caregiver. Maintaining a secure connection with the partner becomes a here-and-now, life or death matter.

Maria's Problems with Self-Assertion

Her Early Losses

Maria struggled with all of the problems discussed above. Her early life had been filled with moments of emotional pain. When she was five, her mother died. After her mother's death, Maria's father paid a neighbor to watch her. The neighbor was an irritable woman who seemed to resent her presence.

Maria didn't understand much of what went on during that period. She didn't understand why her mother died. She didn't know why her father couldn't take care of her. She didn't understand why her neighbor was so irritable. She just knew that she was afraid of antagonizing her father or the neighbor—afraid that they would disappear as well. She adapted by trying to be as sweet and unobtrusive as possible. If she caused no trouble, no one would get angry with her and no one else would leave her.

After the death of her mother things did not return to normal. Her father moved from the Southwest to a large Midwestern city. He was stressed and preoccupied. His time with Maria was limited. She was lucky because she was able to find interested adults elsewhere. She was smart and she worked hard to please her teachers. Her teachers, her neighbors, and her aunts became substitute parents. Unfortunately, these relationships were filled with insecurity. To Maria, one displeasing move and they could instantly withdraw their interest.

As she grew older, other insecurities were layered over her timidity and fear of abandonment. She felt inferior to her school classmates. She didn't have their financial resources and also lacked their self-confidence. She was often startled by their boldness.

Her First Husband: José

Maria won a scholarship to a university in the Midwest. It was there that she met José. He was as outgoing as she was shy. She could never understand why he wanted to date her but was grateful that he did. They went to his fraternity parties and hung out with his friends. If Maria had any needs that were different from José's, neither was aware of them at the time.

Because of José, her time in college was social and exhilarating. She was in love. After her junior year they married. Maria dropped out of college and found a job to support them. As time went on some of the reasons for José's attraction to Maria became clear. José was impulsive and disorganized. Maria stabilized him.

Their Early Clashes:
Maria Yields—José Remains Oblivious

Their marriage became a continuation of the college pattern. Maria was eager to please and fearful of losing José. When they clashed over some difference, Maria quickly yielded. José assumed this was normal.

The Blame/Withdraw/More Blame TRAP Pattern

After college their lives became more complicated and demanding. With children and increased family responsibilities, José's impatience and impulsivity became a problem. When frustrated, he would lash out. If the baby cried, it was Maria's fault. If he was sleep deprived, it was her fault. If they couldn't afford to buy something, it was her fault.

Over the years, José's anger took its toll on Maria. She began to see him as frightening. There was a loss of affection and she began to withdraw. She continued to have sex with him, fearing what would happen if she did not. But she no longer enjoyed their sexual relationship. All that mattered was her children and maintaining a stable home environment. José could not see the connection between his angry blaming and her withdrawal. He just thought she was becoming a cold bitch.

The Lack of Support/Inner Resentment/More Lack of Support TRAP Pattern

Initially, Maria liked the conventional structure of their marriage. José worked. She was responsible for the household and the kids. However, with expenses mounting and the kids all in school, they needed more income. Maria returned to work. Being an employee, wife, and a mother proved to be more than she could handle. She needed help but could not ask for it. Her resentment built. José could see the anger written on her face and in her silent withdrawal. It threatened him, just as his behavior threatened her. The tension increased.

The Parenting Conflict

Maria had more courage when it came to her children. When José's outbursts were directed toward the children, she protected them. José felt undermined. This led to more outbursts. She and the kids began to engage in activities without him. José began to feel like an outsider in his own home. He blamed her for this. In this case he was partially correct; however, he could not see the role he had played in his subsequent isolation from his family.

The TRAP Patterns Kill Their Marriage

The threat level increased. In their guarded postures affection and sex were not possible. They had become enemies. José's extra-marital affairs were inevitable and only created more pain. Despite this, Maria's abandonment fears remained. The thought of the marriage ending terrified Maria. José had no similar fear. He left her for someone else. Maria had another abandonment experience.

Their Failure to Understand the TRAP Patterns

Neither Maria nor José understood much about cause and effect in marriage. If Maria had been more aware of the consequences of her behavior she might have engaged in the following inner dialogue: "If I don't speak up, he will remain oblivious of my needs. He won't help me. Then I will become resentful, see him as selfish, and withdraw. Ultimately that will poison our relationship." Had she been more aware of the consequences of her behavior, perhaps she could have overcome her fear of self-expression and created a more equitable relationship.

José was equally unaware of the consequences of his behavior. He didn't realize that there were two people in the marital bubble. He did not say to himself: "I need to pay attention to her needs as well as mine. If I don't she will become resentful and withdrawn. If this happens, eventually I will be frozen out." Had he thought that way, the marriage might have had a different ending. Both paid the price for their failure to understand the consequences of their behavior. Once they had been in love. However, after too many TRAP patterns they hated each another.

Maria's Second Husband: Miguel

After her divorce, Maria devoted herself to raising her children. Eventually, she met Miguel. They were introduced at a farewell party for a mutual friend who was leaving the Midwest and moving abroad. Maria immediately admired Miguel's intelligence and his basic sense of decency. With Miguel she felt safe. As their relationship developed, she knew that Miguel loved her.

Miguel's Temperament

Miguel was as conflict avoidant as Maria. In his case, it was not based on early losses. There had been no deaths or divorces in his family of origin. However, Miguel had observed the repetitive arguments of his parents and had learned to loath confrontation.

Miguel was an extremely shy and quiet individual. Throughout childhood he was overweight, timid, and teased by schoolmates. There had been significant moments of emotional pain. Much of his time was spent in his room with books and other solitary activities. As an adult he was no longer overweight or timid. Now, others thought Miguel's reserve was snobbishness. They did not realize how uncomfortable he was around people.

Their Marriage and Miguel's Silence

Maria and Miguel's marriage was vulnerable to silent TRAP sequences. Miguel's tendency to be non-communicative was Step 1 in the TRAP sequence. It caused an instant fear response within Maria. When she assumed he was angry, she withdrew in self-protection. This became Step 2. Miguel then responded with his own withdrawal. Convinced that no one could really accept him, he closed himself off at Step 3. The marital bubble became dark, heavy, and oppressive.

Maria Comes Alone For Therapy

Maria came to therapy after finding herself in the worst possible circumstance for someone who fears disapproval. She was caught between Miguel's wishes and those of her daughter. Pleasing one meant displeasing the other. This was creating anxiety and insomnia for Maria.

Maria's daughter had invited her for a visit but wanted her to come alone. The daughter was uncomfortable with Miguel. Maria knew Miguel did not want her to go without him although he would not say so. Caught in the middle, she became increasingly upset. Maria wanted to go alone. But she was terrified of telling him.

Assertiveness Training

Initially, Maria and the therapist worked on helping her express herself. To do so, she had to expose herself to what she feared. She had to speak up and experience that there would be no catastrophe—no one would abandon her, nothing calamitous would happen. On the contrary, when spouses speak up, there is more information present in the relationship. This makes it easier to resolve the issue.

When Maria became fearful of expressing herself, her first and second husbands seemed the same to her: frightening. In reality, the difference was huge. Her first husband was not interested in pleasing her. Miguel was. It was likely that if she gathered up her courage and spoke up, Miguel would be responsive.

In the therapy sessions Maria worked on clarifying what she wanted to say to her husband. She and the therapist rehearsed what she would say. They refined it. They discussed her fears. The conversations went like this:

Therapist: Tell me again what you want to say to him.

Maria: I want to tell him that I want to go alone.

Therapist: What else do you want to say?

Maria: I want him to understand that it is tense when we are all together. I can't relax and enjoy my daughter.

Therapist: How do you want to say that?

They rehearse how she will to say it.

Therapist: What did that feel like?

Maria: It felt uncomfortable.

Therapist: How so?

Maria: What if he gets angry? What if he shuts down and won't speak to me? He never says anything as it is.

Therapist: He knows you love your daughter. He also knows it is uncomfortable when you are all together. My guess is he will understand.

After more sleepless nights Maria eventually spoke up. When she did, there was no catastrophe. Miguel acquiesced. He was a reasonable man.

Getting More Information in the Bubble: More Assertiveness with Miguel

After her initial act of self-assertion, Maria felt better. But she knew her work had just begun. She had many other things to say to Miguel. Maria made a list of the things she wanted to discuss. Here are some of them:

- He left his clothes on the floor.
- He left dishes in the sink.
- They only went where he wanted to go.
- He didn't consult her when making his plans.
- He didn't interact with her children.
- She wanted him to go to church with her.

In each case the withdraw/withdraw TRAP pattern prevailed. What he unknowingly did to upset Maria was Step 1. At Step 2 Maria would say nothing, become resentful and withdraw. At Step 3 Miguel reacted to her withdrawal with his own withdrawal. Silence prevailed. Neither could break it.

Maria and the therapist worked on speaking up about these issues. They discussed what she wanted to say. They rehearsed it. They refined it. They practiced it again.

They also used the downward arrow technique to help her overcome her fear of speaking up.

Overcoming Fear Using the Downward Arrow Technique

The downward arrow technique comes from Cognitive Behavioral Therapy. It is based on the idea that our distress comes from the distorted and exaggerated way in which we talk to ourselves. The downward arrow technique helps spouses become aware of this exaggerated self-talk and helps correct it. The result is less fear.

Keeping a Thought Diary

Spouses are asked to keep a diary of what they are thinking during stressful interactions with the partner.

Evaluating the Thoughts

Later, after each thought has been recorded, the spouse examines it. As each thought is examined the spouse asks, "What am I afraid will happen next?" This elicits still deeper fears about the issue. The technique helps get to the bottom of what the fear is actually about.

The spouse then goes back and evaluates each thought. How realistic or unrealistic is it? What evidence is there to support the validity of the thought? What evidence is there against the validity of the thought?

Doing this can help the spouses begin to grasp the unrealistic nature of the thoughts that underlie their fears.

Maria's Downward Arrow Exercise

The therapist asked Maria to write what she thinks about when she considers telling Miguel what is bothering her. After each thought, she asks herself, "What am I afraid will happen then?" This is what she wrote:

1. If I say what is bothering me he will get upset.

    What am I afraid will happen then?

2. He won't speak to me.

    What am I afraid will happen then?

3. He will always be mad at me.

    What am I afraid will happen then?

4. He will want to end the marriage.

    What am I afraid will happen then?

5. I will be alone.

    What am I afraid will happen then?

6. I will always be alone and unhappy.

Maria Evaluates the Validity of Her Thoughts

Maria considered the validity of each thought. She wrote down evidence for and against each thought. This is what she wrote:

The Thought	Evidence For The Thought	Evidence Against The Thought
If I say what is bothering me he will get angry. *What am I afraid will happen*	My first husband would get angry if I said what was bothering me.	Miguel is not like my first husband. Miguel wants to please me.
I am afraid that he won't speak to me. *What am I afraid will happen*	He is so silent now. It could get worse.	He says he wants me to tell him what I want.
I am afraid that he will always be mad at me. *What am I afraid happen*	It just feels like it could last forever.	He says his silence doesn't mean he is mad. He says he is just quiet.
I am afraid that he will want to end the relationship. *What am I afraid will happen*	All my relationships end.	He pursued me. He loves me. He wants to be with me. He gets lonely without me.
I am afraid that I will be alone. *What am I afraid will happen*	Unpleasant people end up alone.	I would still have my children and my friends. I won't be alone.
I am afraid that I will always be alone and unhappy.	That is my fate.	Sometimes I enjoy being alone. I like reading and sewing. I could handle being alone.

Maria Speaks Up

Maria found this downward arrow exercise helpful. Writing down her inner thoughts and seeing them in the light of day helped her see how unrealistic her fear was. It helped her acquire the courage to speak up. She did speak up about her issues. Again, there was no catastrophe. Maria began to feel better.

Relapse: Maria Says Nothing about Her Knee

Like any behavior change, progress follows a jagged course. Success will be followed by relapse. In this case, the relapse had to do with how they spent their time together. Hiking was an important part of Miguel's life. He was fond of going to his cabin on weekends and hiking. Maria was less enthusiastic. She had an arthritic knee. Too much hiking became painful for her. However, she felt guilty about complaining. She didn't want to spoil Miguel's weekends. Miguel knew nothing about the problem. Maria needed to speak up.

The therapist felt that it was time to include Miguel in the sessions.

Maria and Miguel Unite To Kill the Silent TRAP Pattern

Altering TRAP patterns is more effective when both parties can each work on their contribution to the pattern. Husbands often dislike coming to marital therapy. They are less relationship oriented. They are less comfortable discussing their feelings. This was true of Miguel. But Miguel wanted his marriage to last. He was willing to participate.

Getting More Information into the Marital Bubble by Asking, "Are You Upset?"

When Maria and Miguel appeared for the session, they were uncomfortable. When the therapist asked about the problems in their relationship, there was silence. When the therapist probed, he got halting responses. Each was afraid of upsetting the other. It did not feel safe to begin.

Eventually, Maria began. She said there was too much silence in their relationship. It made her anxious. She gave an example. The incident began when she called a plumber to fix a faucet. Miguel seemed annoyed. "What was wrong with the faucet?" Miguel had asked. Maria became distressed. She feared that she had done something to displease him. "He hates spending money," she thought. She berated herself and withdrew.

Miguel could see that Maria was upset. But he was too closed off to ask why. He feared a confrontation and remained silent. To Maria, Miguel's silence meant that he was angry. The silence continued for some time.

Was Miguel Angry? More Murky Marital Reality

During the session, Miguel was surprised to learn that Maria thought he was angry. "I wasn't angry," he told her. He merely wanted to know more about the leaky faucet. Murky marital reality was setting in. Was his *Protector* keeping him from acknowledging that that he was angry? "Would 'annoyed' be a better word?" the therapist asked. How about mildly irritated? Miguel said he was feeling none of those things.

The therapist was dubious. Miguel's *Protector* seemed to be in control. Despite Miguel's denial regarding his anger, Maria appeared relieved. At least they were discussing the issue. The tense silence had been broken.

Asking: "Is Anything Bothering You?"

As they discussed the withdraw/withdraw TRAP pattern, they began to see how each was reacting to the other. They wanted to break this pattern and were willing to make the effort to change. If one noticed that the other had withdrawn they agreed to ask, "Is something bothering you?"

They also agreed to try to answer honestly, even if the answer was "yes." Sharing negative feelings was frightening for both of them, but they appeared to understand the importance of doing so. They were beginning to understand the necessity of speaking up.

Following Up on "Is Anything Bothering You?"

Maria seemed more motivated to ask the "Is anything bothering you?" question. Over the course of several months she asked the question repeatedly. Usually, his answer was, "No." Did nothing ever upset Miguel? Was Miguel never angry? It seemed unlikely. *Protector* was creating some murkiness in the situation. But the mere act of asking the question and getting any answer relieved Maria. It helped her to avoid withdrawal.

Getting More Information in the Bubble: Being Better Talkers and Listeners

During another session the therapist asked how their time together had been. Miguel looked at Maria. Maria looked at Miguel. There was silence. Eventually Maria broke the silence. She said that the week had gone well. The therapist looked at Miguel. "What has it been like for you?" the therapist asked. He said things were fine. They fell into another silence. It was not a tense silence, but it was a silence nevertheless. There was an absence of information and energy in their marital bubble. If this continued, eventually the relationship would become apathetic and lifeless.

Maria complained that she knew little about Miguel's work life. She didn't know how he spent his day, nor did she know much about his work colleagues. When she asked him about his day, he would reply, "Work was fine."

The therapist asked Miguel about his work. Miguel said there was not much to tell. He said that it was all technical. The therapist asked more questions. Eventually Miguel began to open up. As he did the room became filled with energy. "This is interesting. Why don't you share any of this with your wife?" the therapist asked.

Miguel: "I don't think she is interested."

Therapist: "What makes you say that?"

Miguel: (Bitterly). "Why would anyone be interested?"

Therapist (to Maria): "What do you make of this?"

Maria said that she was interested. She appeared to be sincere. "Why do you think Miguel feels this way?" the therapist asked.

Fear of Self-Disclosure

Miguel was afraid of self-disclosure. He had never shared his inner life with anyone. No one in his family of origin had showed much interest, nor had anyone else. Not that Miguel had given anyone much of a chance. He was afraid of being evaluated and laughed at. As a result, he felt safe but isolated. He didn't want it to be this way; he just thought it was inevitable.

As the conversation continued it appeared that Maria was equally convinced that Miguel wasn't interested in the details of her life. She said that Miguel often appeared bored when she related the events of her day.

Their Assignment: Be a Good Talker and a Good Listener

The therapist gave them an assignment. Each day, Miguel was to tell Maria something about his work day. Maria's job was to be a good listener. Since any form of self-disclosure was difficult for Miguel, it was crucial that Maria show interest. Then they were then to switch roles. Maria was to tell Miguel about her day. Miguel was to be the interested listener.

For many, this would be an easy task. For Miguel and Maria it was filled with risk. Miguel was highly sensitive to perceived disinterest. He was also a heavy editor of his own thoughts. Most of what he thought about he deemed unworthy of communicating.

Following Up: The Talking/Listening Task Went Well

Miguel worked hard to be a good listener. Maria would share the events of her day and Miguel would try to be attentive. Maria noticed and was appreciative. As a talker Miguel struggled. He wanted to become less introverted; however, sharing the events of his daily life was not easy for this highly private man. Miguel and the therapist discussed this.

Miguel: Sometimes my mind is just blank. She will say, "What are you thinking about?" I am not thinking about anything.

Therapist: I don't think your mind is blank. You just decide your thoughts are unworthy of sharing and you edit them out.

After considering this, Miguel agreed. He realized he had many thoughts and some of them were not kind. They were full of severe judgments about others. Despite this, Miguel worked to overcome his self-editing. In small, but significant ways, he shared more about his family, his bosses, his co-workers, his projects, his photography and his aspirations for their relationship. When he did so, he realized that there was no catastrophe. No one laughed at him. No one judged him. Maria was a good listener. The amount of information in the bubble was increasing. The threat level was going down.

The TRAP Sequence Fades Away

Maria and Miguel were successful in overcoming the silent TRAP sequence that dominated their relationship. They remained quiet, reserved people. But now, when there was silence in their marital bubble, it lacked the earlier tension. There was enough information in the bubble to enable them to feel safe with one another. Maria could ask Miguel if he was mad at her and Miguel would give her enough information to allow her to relax. They understood the consequences of not speaking up and were determined to avoid them. Maria's fears of abandonment receded. The marital bubble was no longer so dark and oppressive.

Is Your Marriage Dominated By Silent TRAP Sequences?

Is your marriage like Maria and Miguel's? If it is then try doing the things that Maria and Miguel did. Fill out the rating scales and identify your threatening behaviors. Identify the TRAP sequences. Complete the assertiveness exercise. Consider trying the downward arrow technique.

Try to increase your awareness of what goes on in your relationship. Monitor yourself for conflict avoidance. Identify the choice points. Consider the consequences of withdrawing and not speaking up. Notice what happens when you do and when you don't. If things begin to improve, try to understand why. If you begin to make progress, be prepared for the ups and downs—and persevere.

Exercise 13: Assertiveness

What do I want to say that I am afraid to say?

_____

_____

_____

_____

_____

How do I feel about myself if I say the above?

_____

_____

_____

Do I feel guilty if I speak up? If so, list the evidence for and the evidence against the idea that I should feel guilty.

Evidence For   Evidence Against

_____   _____

_____   _____

_____   _____

Do I feel unequal and not entitled to speak up? If so, list the evidence for and the evidence against the idea that I am unequal and not entitled to speak up.

Evidence For   Evidence Against

_____   _____

_____   _____

_____   _____

Do I fear that I will be disapproved of? If so, list the evidence for and the evidence against the idea that I will be disapproved of.

Evidence For   Evidence Against

_____   _____

_____   _____

_____   _____

Do I fear that I will be abandoned? If so, list evidence for and evidence against the idea that I will be abandoned.

Evidence For   Evidence Against

_____   _____

_____   _____

_____   _____

How can I state what I'm afraid to say? Avoid derogatory language. Include no zingers, putdowns, or accusations.

_____

_____

_____

_____

Practice saying it until it feels comfortable.

10	Anita and Garrison Deal With A Jealousy/Anger TRAP

Fig. 10-1: The importance of a solid foundation

Trust: The Foundation for Marriage

Mistrust and Irresponsible Behavior

Trust is the foundation upon which all else in marriage rests. Nothing leads to arguments faster than behavior that creates mistrust. Some mistrust TRAP patterns are based on irresponsible behavior. Knowing that the behavior is irresponsible, the spouse tries to conceal it.

The irresponsible behavior might be an addiction—drinking, drugging, or gambling. It might be foolish spending or not paying the bills. It might be sexual infidelity. When irresponsibility is the issue, the TRAP pattern is as follows: Step 1—the spouse behaves irresponsibly. Step 2—the partner accuses the spouse of acting irresponsibly. Step 3— the spouse becomes defensive and lies about the irresponsible behavior. This leads to more TRAP sequences and an escalating argument.

Mistrust of Innocuous Behavior

Other mistrust TRAP patterns are jealousy based and begin more innocently. At Step 1 there is an innocuous behavior that is perceived as threatening. The spouse may be paying too much attention to something or someone else—or so the jealous partner thinks. The spouse may want to spend time with his parents, meet his friends for a drink, or wash his car. The insecure partner will feel unduly threatened by this loss of attention and become jealous. At Step 2 the jealous partner makes an angry accusation. In essence the partner says, "You like this other person or activity more than you like me!" The spouse feels besieged with questions and suspicion. At Step 3 the spouse denies the accusation, sometimes with the implication that the partner is imagining things or is crazy. This becomes the trigger for the next round in the escalating argument.

Hoping to ward off more suspicious questions about how he is spending his time, the spouse may become secretive about his activities. The attempts at secrecy usually fail and now the partner's mistrust is based on the spouse's concealment of his actions as well as the innocuous behavior itself. The mistrust grows.

The combination of a jealous partner and a secretive spouse is a dangerous mix. Yet jealous and secretive people seem to find one another. They do appear to have one thing in common. They share a distrustful view of the world.

Why Are People Jealous?

Jealousy may be biologically hardwired. It may have been an adaptive emotion that developed throughout evolution. By identifying sexual competitors and eliminating them through attack, partners could not only protect what was theirs, but also maintain the cohesiveness of the family unit, thus insuring the survival of the young.

As with other primitive, negative emotions, in the modern world jealousy does more harm than good. It does harm because the jealous spouse cannot attack and eliminate a sexual rival. Instead, the jealous spouse attacks the motives of the partner, thus creating threat within the marriage.

The Threatening Other

In marriage, the perceived threat is not restricted to sexual competitors. Partners can become jealous of almost anything that the spouse seems to care about. The threatening "other" could be the partner's work or hobby; the partner's desire to read the newspaper or watch TV; or jog. If the partner devotes too much attention to the "other," the spouse concludes: "You must like the 'other' more than you like me." Reaching this conclusion activates abandonment fears for some. For others it creates doubts about self-worth.

Thinking in Threes: "Us" versus "Them"

Those vulnerable to jealousy often interject a third person into the marital dyad. They think in terms of three person systems rather than two person systems. To feel secure the spouse must unite with the partner against the threatening third person. It is not just you and me—it is you and me together against him or her. The spouses must comprise the "us" and third figure must be the "them," the enemy. If there is no real enemy to unite against, then the insecure spouse may create one.

To some degree, all of us are prone to this kind of thinking. We draw boundaries around our loved ones. Those within the boundaries are the good people; those outside the boundaries are more questionable. This us-them thinking sometimes has trivial consequences. It is harmless if Ohio State football fans congregate in bars together and cheer against Michigan or vice versa. It is less trivial if conservatives and liberals see each other as the enemy and can find no common ground. The results are more profound if religious or national differences result in perceived enemies and war.

In marriage, loyalty becomes everything when such thinking is present. If the spouse invests too much time or energy in someone or something else, this is seen as an act of betrayal. This puts great pressure on the non-jealous spouse to also see the world in terms of friends and enemies. If he or she does not, the result is perceived as betrayal.

Why Do People Lie?

Lying creates mistrust. Lying is also based on mistrust. People who lie assume that bad things will happen if they are open and honest. Like their jealous partners, they doubt the good intentions of others. They see others as naturally unresponsive and oppositional. They assume that people are out for themselves. Thus, in order to get what they want, they must be deceitful.

In other instances people do not lie in order to get something. They lie to avoid something. They can't tolerate the anticipated angry reaction of the partner when they tell the truth. They don't like feeling that they must lie; however, they see it as better than the alternative—telling the truth and dealing with the negative consequences.

Let's consider these issues with regard to Anita.

Anita's Family Background

Anita had experienced more than her share of emotional pain. Lying, distrust, and divorce had been an integral part of Anita's family background. Her parents had both worked in the airline industry in the Northwest when they met. Both were unhappily married and would commiserate over lunches together. Eventually, they had an affair and left their former spouses for each other. Anita was their biological child.

As a child Anita listened to her anguished mother accuse her father of infidelity. She listened to her father's vehement denials. He accused her mother of imagining things and over-reacting. But her mother was not imagining his affairs. Despite his denials, they were real.

Anita came to see the world through her mother's eyes. There were always third parties involved in marriage—other women hovering over the household wanting to cause trouble. When her father eventually left the family, the unseen enemy had won. As a child Anita swore that this would never happen to her.

For years after the divorce her ex-husband became her mother's enemy and it was clear to whom Anita must be loyal. When she visited her father and enjoyed herself, she felt guilty. However, these moments were rare. Mostly, she felt ignored. His new wife's children were competitors who seemed to get more of her father's attention than she did.

Other three-person relationships followed. In school there were girlfriends who were loyal to you and those whom you couldn't trust. There were girls who would talk behind your back or worse, girls who wanted to steal your boyfriend. Later there were work conflicts. There were colleagues who were on your side and others who wanted to make you look bad. Anita hated the politics of the work environment. Yet, she was always in the middle of the intrigue.

Anita's First Marriage

As is often the case, jealous and devious people seem to find one another. So it was with Anita and George. She was jealousy prone; he was full of secrets. George had charisma. He was part of the music scene in the Northwest. Anita was attracted to him. She was also flattered; of all the women that he could be with, he had chosen her.

Before marriage, their relationship had been tempestuous. George would get high with his friends and not tell her. He would see other women and lie about it. Anita would find out and become furious. They would break up, only to get back together. Eventually, they married.

Why did Anita marry George? She knew he wasn't trustworthy. She knew he lied.

(1) Did she accept lying as normal? Did she believe that all men lied?

(2) Did she think her love would change him?

(3) Did she think he would settle down after they got married?

(4) Was she trying to change the ending of her parents' marriage?

(5) Did she think that a lying husband was all she was entitled to?

Anita couldn't say for sure.

George did try to be a good husband, and for a while it worked. However, George was not prepared for the restrictions of marriage. In giving up his former lifestyle, he felt like he was losing the best part of himself. He began to do his own thing. Unfortunately, doing his own thing was not good for George. He wasted money. He drank too much. He was in internet chat rooms and on porn web sites.

Did George want to stay married? He definitely did. Was George thinking about how to stay married? He definitely was not. He was not thinking about the consequences of his behavior. He had little aware-ness of choice points. George was just doing *what he wanted to do when he wanted to do it.*

All of his irresponsible behaviors became Step 1 in their TRAP sequences. At Step 2 Anita would confront him about his actions. At Step 3 he would deny them. Their arguments would quickly escalate. On several occasions, Anita would tell George to leave. When he did so, Anita's abandonment fears became intense and she would want him back. George would admit that he had lied and promise to do better. She would take him back.

The pattern would begin again. Anita began to obsess about what George was doing. She monitored his email, looked at his phone records, went over his credit cards purchases, and checked his pockets. But there were always new credit cards, new phone cards, and new mailboxes.

Her obsessing and their arguing took a toll on Anita's health. She worried constantly. She had insomnia. She was chronically angry. She was losing weight. George had become the enemy. Finally, her stress and deteriorating health outweighed her abandonment concerns. She ended the marriage for good.

Anita's Second Marriage

Anita's second marriage was to Garrison. Unlike her first husband, Garrison was not looking for excitement. Garrison was an engineer and a workaholic. Mainly, what he wanted was to focus on his work and then spend time with his wife. They had spent many hours together fishing the waters of the Northwest.

Garrison had been married before. His divorce had been quite painful. There were legal battles over custody, visitation, and child support. Anita had helped Garrison through these battles. Inadver-tently, his legal struggles had brought them together. They were united against his evil ex-wife. But that was in the past. Now their unity was threatened by Anita's insecurity. Sometimes she didn't know whose side Garrison was on.

When Garrison stayed late at work, Anita felt a moment of emotional pain—she thought he preferred his work to her. When he traveled for work she experienced a moment of emotional pain—she thought that he preferred being off in distant cities and fancy restaur-ants. When he had to communicate with his ex-wife, she experienced a moment of emotional pain. She wondered if he still had feelings for his ex-wife. When they went with his children to visit his mother, she experienced a moment of emotional pain. She felt like an outsider. When he looked at other women, she experienced a moment of emotional pain. Were they more attractive than she was? Did he prefer them?

Garrison was paying the price for Anita's early experiences of loss and betrayal. Garrison thought her fears were ridiculous. He was normally an affable man. But when he felt cornered by her accusations he would lash out with hurtful remarks that elicited TRAP sequences. At other times he would ignore her and retreat into himself. This also led to TRAP sequences. Consider the following interaction:

Their Derogatory Arguments

That morning there had been a number of minor skirmishes that resulted in Anita feeling ignored. However, the obvious trigger for the TRAP sequence occurred as they were leaving home. As Anita waited by the door, Garrison dawdled in front of his laptop, reading his work email. This elicited a moment of emotional pain—a feeling that she was being ignored again. It felt like he preferred his work to her.

Anita: "I am waiting for you! Can't pull yourself away from your computer? Why am I so unimportant to you?"

If Anita had focused solely on the issue of his lateness, perhaps he would have listened. But she made a more general accusation: that he considered her unimportant. This bothered him. With the aid of Protector, he concluded that she was being ridiculous again. Acting on this attitude he made a derogatory remark.

Garrison: "Stop being an idiot. I was just checking my work email."

Calling Anita an idiot was offensive. It caused another moment of emotional pain. Now Anita became angrier and more determined to prove her point.

Anita: "You know you would rather be at work, where they all treat you like a god."

Anita feels threatened by his work colleagues. Garrison is successful at his job and his colleagues admire his accomplishments. He also respects and likes them. To Anita, this is a threat to their bond with each other.

Garrison does not understand this. What he does understand is that he feels wrongly accused of craving his coworkers' admiration. As his anger mounts, his language becomes rougher.

Garrison: "That is bullshit."

The words "idiot" and "bullshit" have set the tone. They prompt Anita to join the derogatory language club.

Anita: "They all kiss your ass and you love it."

The idea that he wants people to kiss his ass infuriates Garrison. He escalates the level of derogation.

Garrison: "Anita, why are you acting like such a bitch?"

The accusation that she is a bitch moves the argument to a new level of distress. More derogatory language follows. Their afternoon together is ruined.

Identifying Derogatory Language

In piecing together the steps of their argument, the therapist asked for the specific language they used with one another. They were embarrassed. Their *Protectors* resisted. It was disturbing for them to admit that they used words like bitch, ass, bullshit, and idiot. Although the therapist managed to unearth some of their language, at some point their *Protectors* won. The therapist suspected that there was even more hurtful language used that day that they would not admit to.

What did they think was going to happen when they used such words? the therapist asked. How did they think their partner would react? It was clear that, during the argument, they hadn't thought about it. If they had thought about it, they wouldn't have done it. The task became to focus more on monitoring their behavior and on anticipating the consequences of using such words.

Exercise 14: Identifying Derogatory Words

List all the derogatory words you and your spouse used during your last argument.

_____   _____

_____   _____

_____   _____

_____   _____

_____   _____

_____   _____

_____   _____

_____   _____

They Commit to Editing Out Derogation

Editing out derogatory language is not easy. When people are upset, it is one of *Protector's* favorite devices. However, with awareness, self-monitoring, and recognition of the consequences, it is possible to gain self-control. After several months of effort, and with the predictable instances of progress and relapse, Anita and Garrison had some success. As they began to recognize the futility of using derogatory language, it became easier. *Protector* did not like this. *Protector* had lost a weapon. But *Protector* was no longer in control.

The TRAP Sequence Based on Concealment

Garrison often lied to Anita. Or perhaps "conceal" would be a better word. He wasn't secretive in order to get something. He had most of what he wanted. He lied because he dreaded his wife's angry accusations and wanted to avoid them at all costs. The sequence went as follows:

1. Garrison has a business lunch with a woman colleague.
2. Garrison leaves this fact out of his conversation Anita.
3. Anita finds out and becomes angry.
4. Garrison tries to explain away his secretiveness but fails.
5. Anita becomes more distrustful.
6. Garrison becomes more guarded and secretive.
7. Anita becomes more insecure.

Another variation on this theme went as follows:

1. Garrison must work late.
2. Garrison fears his wife's angry response to his working late.
3. Garrison calls and says he will be home in an hour. In reality, it will be three hours.
4. When he shows up after three hours Anita is furious.
5. "Why did he lie? What is he hiding?" she wonders.
6. Garrison becomes more guarded.
7. Anita becomes more insecure.

They Work to Overcome the Secretive TRAP Sequence

As they analyze the sequence they begin to recognize how each contributed to it. Anita's angry reaction caused Garrison to conceal.

Garrison's concealment caused Anita to become suspicious. They wanted to break out of this rut.

Anita said that she wanted Garrison to be honest. Garrison said that he wanted to be honest, but he feared her angry reaction. "If you get mad at what I tell you, then I won't tell you," he said. Anita struggled with this. She could recognize cause and effect, she just didn't like it. In the interest of his becoming more open, she agreed to try to control her angry reaction.

Garrison, warily, began to take the risk of greater openness. He told her about his work interactions with women. He tried to be more honest about when he is coming home. Anita prepared herself for these conversations. She considered what inner dialogue she might use to help remain calm. She settled on: "He loves me. He is just trying to do his job." When she felt herself becoming upset, she used this inner dialogue. At the choice point she was better able to control herself. Both were relieved.

Garrison Engaged in Perspective-Taking

In the past, with the aid of *Protector*, Garrison would deny Anita's accusations and conclude that she was crazy. This, temporarily, helped him feel better. After discussions with therapist, he tried to get beyond this *Protector* driven response and began to engage in perspective-taking.

Instead of defensively denying her charges, he tried to consider her inner experience. "Why would she feel this way?" he asked himself. He began to consider her early experiences with other men. She had told him how she had felt ignored by her father. When her father left the family, she blamed herself. "Had I been a more pleasing child would he have stayed?" she wondered. Garrison recalled these conversations. "How how this affected her?" he wondered. Even today, Garrison could see that her father could upset her if he appeared indifferent. "What does that feel like?" he wondered.

Garrison also knew of Anita's first husband's infidelities. They had discussed how painful that period had been. He began to see his wife differently. He began to feel sorry for her. Many men had hurt her. He didn't want to be another one. It wasn't that hard to understand where her insecurity was coming from.

Garrison decided to find ways to help his wife feel that she was number one in his life.

Garrison Worked on Reassurance, Anita Worked on Calming Herself

Garrison Invited Anita to Dinner

Garrison was preparing for an out-of-town presentation. He knew he would be late. He called and told Anita. She was not happy but had prepared herself to accept it. She did not express anger, allowing Garrison to remain calm and non-defensive. It gave him the opportunity to come up with a better idea. Later, he called his wife and asked her to bring takeout food to the office. They can eat together. Driving through rush hour traffic did not appeal to Anita and she declined. Still, she was pleased. Garrison had initiated this. He had made the effort. She felt both wanted and special.

They Went on a Trip Together

Garrison was starting to understand. He wanted her to feel wanted. He wanted her to feel secure. Garrison needed to attend a conference overseas. He asked Anita to come with him. It would be expensive, but they could find the money. Their common goal became to enjoy the trip and return from it still liking one another.

They discussed the potential trouble spots that could create arguments. One was that he will be at meetings all day and she will be on her own. Will she feel ignored? She didn't think so if they agree to meet for lunch each day and tour together when there is time. Another trouble spot would be the group dinners. He had to attend them and interact with other women. Will this create jealousy? Anita agreed that it might.

Anita prepared herself for the group dinners. During the dinners she self-monitored for feelings of jealousy. She tried to use self-validation. She engaged in the same inner dialogue that had helped earlier: "He loves me. He is just trying to do his job."

Garrison also wanted the trip to go well. He knew his wife thought he flirted. He didn't think he did, but he knew that saying so would only lead to a TRAP sequence. He had had enough arguing about this issue. At the dinners he made it a point to stay away from attractive women.

Their trip went well. They succeeded in achieving their goal. They had fun and still liked each other when they returned. Things began improving for Anita and Garrison. They stopped using derogatory language. The jealousy episodes decreased. However, as is usually the case, it is two steps forward, then one step back.

Relapse: They Visit His Mother

Anita didn't like Garrison's mother. She had never felt accepted by her and was uncomfortable around her. When she complained to Garrison about this, her complaints became Step 1 in the ensuing TRAP sequence. Garrison defended his mother. This created an "us versus them" situation for Anita. Garrison appeared to be siding with his mother, leaving Anita in the excluded position. She reacted strongly and the argument escalated.

When they visited his parents, the ritual had been for Garrison to go off and play golf with his father, leaving Anita at home with his mother. Anita wanted Garrison to play golf and felt guilty about preventing it. Thus, she tried to endure his mother, but she was rarely able to. Their arguing often began after Garrison returned from golf and Anita complained about his mother.

On this occasion their argument destroyed all the good will that they had built up in the previous months. They were back in their rut. Anita was angry and Garrison was withdrawn.

Problem-Solving

When both were calm they decided to engage in a problem-solving exercise. They brain-stormed together and came up with ten ways to solve the problem:

1. Anita can stay home when Garrison visits his parents.
2. Anita can play golf with Garrison and his father.
3. Anita can take her mother-in-law shopping.
4. Anita can visit her sister-in-law.
5. Anita can go to the gym.
6. Anita can bring her laptop and work.
7. Anita can read a book.
8. Garrison can stay home and not play golf.
9. Garrison and Anita can go off together.
10. Garrison and Anita can plan a joint activity with his parents.

Anita and Garrison decided that most of the above options had some merit. They began to employ them on subsequent visits. Suddenly, they had a plan. They were working with one another. Anita was no longer in the non-preferred position. They executed their plan with some success. Anita still didn't like Garrison's mother; however, their plan helped minimize the damage. The repetitive argument no longer dominated their visits. They were back on track.

Garrison and Anita continued to have their ups and downs. Jealousy is a primitive and powerful emotion. However, both worked at changing their own behavior and their jealousy-related arguments no longer controlled the relationship.

Is Your Marriage like Anita and Garrison's?

Is your marriage similar to Anita and Garrison's? If so, fill out the rating scales and identify your threatening behaviors. Identify the TRAP sequences. Is your own problematic behavior at Step 1, Step 2 or Step 3?

Consider adopting the approaches presented in this chapter. If you are on the receiving end of jealous accusations, then look for ways to reassure your spouse of the importance you place on the relationship. If you are the jealous spouse, work on a self-affirming inner dialogue.

Try to increase your awareness of what goes on in your relationship. Monitor yourself for the threatening behavior. Identify the choice points. Consider the consequences of your choices. Notice what happens when your choice takes you in one direction or the other. If things begin to improve, try to understand why. If you begin to make progress, be prepared for the ups and downs—and persevere.

Final Words

The goal for this book has been to enable the reader to understand more clearly what occurs during marital arguments. Arguing has been described as a reciprocal process. You influence your partner—your partner influences you. You react to your partner, your partner reacts to you. This has been referred to as a TRAP sequence. Hopefully you now have a greater ability to step away from your marriage, observe the TRAP sequence, and understand what you have been doing to perpetuate it.

If you have been stuck in TRAP sequences, the hope is that you now have new ideas about how to avoid these miserable interactions. The work required to do so is hard. But the result, a more harmonious relationship, is well worth the effort.

Recommended Readings

Beck, A. T. (1988). *Love is never enough: How couples can overcome misunderstandings, resolve conflicts, and solve relationship problems through cognitive therapy.* New York: Harper & Row.

Buss, D. (2000) *Jealousy: The dangerous passion.* The Free Press, New York, N.Y.

Cutrona, C. (2006) *Social support in couples.* Sage Publications, Thousand Oaks, California.

Ferguson, D. (2006). *Reptiles in love: Ending destructive fights and evolving toward more loving relationships.* San Francisco, CA: Jossey-Bass.

Fine, C. (2006). *A mind of its own: How your brain distorts and deceives.* New York: W.W. Norton &.

Fisher, H. (2004) *Why we love.* Henry Holt, New York, N.Y.

Gottman, J. & Silver, N. (1999). *The seven principles for making marriage work.* Three Rivers Press, New York, N.Y.

LeDoux, J. E. (1996). *The emotional brain: The mysterious underpinnings of emotional life.* New York: Simon & Schuster.

Panksepp, J. (1998). *Affective neuroscience: The foundations of human and animal emotions.* Series in affective science. New York: Oxford University Press.

Rugel, R. (2003) *Treating marital stress: Support based approaches.* Haworth Press, Binghamton, N.Y.

Rugel, R. (1997) *Husband-focused marital therapy.* Charles C Thomas, Springfield, Illinois.

Appendix: Additional Forms

The Support List

What Kind of Support Do You Want From Your Partner?

1. Parenting

_____

_____

_____

2. Household Chores

_____

_____

_____

3. Communication

_____

_____

_____

4. In-Laws

_____

_____

_____

5. Alone Time

_____

_____

_____

6. Sex Life

_____

_____

_____

7. Companionship Activities

_____

_____

_____

8. Finances

_____

_____

_____

9. Other

_____

_____

_____

Assessing Inner Thoughts and Fears Regarding Assertiveness

If you have assertiveness issues consider using the following to evaluate the evidence for and against your thoughts regarding self-assertion.

Thought	Evidence For	Evidence Against
What Am I Afraid Would Happen Then?		
What Am I Afraid Would Happen Then?		
What Am I Afraid Would Happen Then?		
What Am I Afraid Would Happen Then?		
What Am I Afraid Would Happen Then?		
What Am I Afraid Would Happen Then?		

The Problem-Solving List

Identify the Problem

_____

_____

_____

Develop 8 possible solutions to the problem

1. _____

    _____

    _____

2. _____

    _____

    _____

3. _____

    _____

    _____

4. _____

    _____

    _____

5. _____

    _____

    _____

6. _____

    _____

    _____

7. _____

_____

_____

8. _____

_____

_____

Choose the best solutions

_____

_____

_____

_____

_____

Marital Rating Scales

Rate Your Partner and Yourself on the Following Dimensions

Being unsupportive and disregarding	None	A Little	Moderate Amount	Significant Amount	Severe Amount
You	1	2	3	4	5
Your Partner	1	2	3	4	5

Being critical and derogatory	None	A Little	Moderate Amount	Significant Amount	Severe Amount
You	1	2	3	4	5
Your Partner	1	2	3	4	5

Being controlling and coercive	None	A Little	Moderate Amount	Significant Amount	Severe Amount
You	1	2	3	4	5
Your Partner	1	2	3	4	5

Being withdrawing and avoidant	None	A Little	Moderate Amount	Significant Amount	Severe Amount
You	1	2	3	4	5
Your Partner	1	2	3	4	5

Being angry and impulsive	None	A Little	Moderate Amount	Significant Amount	Severe Amount
You	1	2	3	4	5
Your Partner	1	2	3	4	5

Being jealous and insecure	None	A Little	Moderate Amount	Significant Amount	Severe Amount
You	1	2	3	4	5
Your Partner	1	2	3	4	5

Being secretive and lying	None	A Little	Moderate Amount	Significant Amount	Severe Amount
You	1	2	3	4	5
Your Partner	1	2	3	4	5

Scoring the Marital Rating Scales

For each of the seven threatening behaviors enter your rating of yourself, and your partner's rating of you, in the appropriate box in the table below. Then, add your ratings to your partner's ratings to get a total score for each behavior. Enter the total score in the box labeled "Total." If you are doing the ratings alone, just use your own ratings.

	Unsupportive Disregarding	Critical Derogatory	Controlling Coercive	Withdrawing Avoidant	Angry Impulsive	Jealous Insecure	Lying Secretive
Your Rating of Yourself							
Your Partner's Rating of You							
Total							

	Unsupportive Disregarding	Critical Derogatory	Controlling Coercive	Withdrawing Avoidant	Angry Impulsive	Jealous Insecure	Lying Secretive
Your Rating of Your Partner							
Your Partner's Rating of Self							
Total							

Plot the total score for each threatening behavior on the threat profile below.

What is your most elevated area? This is the area in which you are creating the most threat in the marital bubble. It is the way you are contributing to the TRAP pattern. It is what you need to work on.

Another way to determine what to work on is to have your partner fill out the "What Bothers Me the Most about My Partner" scale. Use these ratings to determine which behaviors you need to work on

Perceived Threat Level

Perceived Threat level	Unsupportive Disregarding	Critical Derogatory	Controlling Coercive	Withdrawing Avoidant	Angry Impulsive	Jealous Insecure	Lying Secretive
10							
9							
8							
7							
6							
5							
4							
3							
2							
1							

What bothers me the most about my partner...

	Bothers me a little	Bothers me a lot	Bothers me the most
My partner's disregard and lack of support	1	2	3
My partner's derogation and criticism	1	2	3
My partner's control and coercion	1	2	3
My partner's withdrawal and avoidance	1	2	3
My partner's anger and impulsivity	1	2	3
My partner's jealousy and insecurity	1	2	3
My partner's lying and secretiveness	1	2	3

About the Author

Robert P. Rugel, PhD grew up in suburban Philadelphia. For over 35 years, Dr. Rugel has worked with couples in his clinical practice. He has also taught courses in marital therapy, supervised graduate students in marital therapy, and conducted marital therapy outcome research at George Mason University where he is now Associate Professor Emeritus. He is the author three previous books: *Dealing with the Problem of Low Self-Esteem* (Charles C Thomas, 1995); *Husband-Focused Marital Therapy* (Charles C Thomas, 1997); and, *Treating Marital Stress* (Haworth Press, 2003).

Dr. Rugel is always looking for more effective ways to help couples. The concepts and metaphors in the present book are his latest attempt present understandable ideas that can help troubled spouses improve their marriages.

Hopefully, reading this book will help spouses will understand why arguments occur, i.e. how they threaten and become threatened by their partners, how they attempt to protect themselves in destructive ways, and how they can avoid these negative, escalating interactions.

In the future, Dr. Rugel will continue to work with couples, write books, go to the movies with his wife, and in his spare time pursue his quest to become an average golfer.

Index

Psychology : Psychotherapy - Couples & Family $19.95 / £10.95

Essentials of Premarital Counseling

Sandra L. Ceren, PhD

Expand Your Clinical Practice with this Practical Hands-on Guide

- Teach conflict resolution skills to your couples
- Introspective quizzes expose more of couples' inner lives and past history to each other
- Real-life exercises let couples practice cooperative decision-making and compromise *before* a crisis happens.
- Couples will discover and have the opportunity to change bad habits which threaten the viability of the relationship.

Therapists Acclaim for *Essentials of Pre-Marital Counseling*

"An invaluable ten-week program of specific steps to evaluate a relationship, detect warning signs and avoid disastrous pitfalls before committing to marriage."   —Holly A. Hunt, PhD
author of *Essentials of Private Practice*

"What I find most rewarding about this book is what Dr. Ceren refers to as 'The art of gracious compromise'-or what may be called-how to get along in your relationship. Therapists take heed, this book is for you and your clients! You will benefit greatly."
—Michael J. Salamon, Ph.D., FICPP
Senior Psychologist/Director, Adult Developmental Center
Author of *The Shidduch Crisis*

"A remarkable roadmap to a healthy relationship and insight into self, written by a therapist who combines experience and skill in improving the lives of others."   —Rosalee G. Weiss, PhD
Diplomate, American Board of Psychological Specialties

www.DrSandraLevyCeren.com

BOOK #7 IN THE
NEW HORIZONS
IN THERAPY
SERIES

Loving Healing Press

Got An Angry Kid? Parenting Spike a Seriously Difficult Child
ISBN 978-1-932690-89-7
More information at www.DrAGibson.com

✗ Does your family live in conflict?

✗ Does your child have a psychiatric label (such as ADHD, oppositional defiance, conduct disorder, bi-polar disorder) or the behavior that would get him/her one?

✗ Have you lost (or nearly lost) control of your child?

If you answered YES to any of these three things, then P.A.C.T. can help you as it has helped thousands of other families restore love and integrity to their relationships!

What Others Say About *Got An Angry Kid?* and The Parenting Angry Children and Teens (P.A.C.T.) Training Program

"The family is much calmer. Taking P.A.C.T. Training was the best decision I ever made. It's the best hard work I've ever done. P.A.C.T. was the light at the end of the tunnel for us."
– Ms. K. D., Willimantic, CT, Mom and Dad of an adolescent girl placed in foster care

"From my professional experience as a manager in the field, P.A.C.T. is one of the very few services which has been held in high regard by our professional staff as well as the families which benefitted from Dr. Gibson's excellent program."
– Ms. Helen Lawrence (retired) Connecticut State Department of Children and Families (CTSDCF)

"I have had to fight for every service for my family. P.A.C.T. is my best chance to [create] change. Thanks for everything."
– Ms. K.M., Vernon, CT, single Mom of an out-of-control son

"Although I was only a few weeks into P.A.C.T., I felt myself becoming calmer, more hopeful, and more in control. P.A.C.T. is putting life into my parenting and does what three years of residential placement didn't."
– Mrs D.W., Hamden, CT, single Mom of a seriously emotionally disturbed boy

"Again, I can't say enough about how this program has changed my life."
– Mr. L.C., New Milford, CT, single parent of a foster child

"P.A.C.T. and *Got An Angry Kid?* is brilliant."
– Parenting consultant

For more information, visit www.DrAGibson.com

Loving Healing Press